Am I teaching well?

Self-Evaluation Strategies for Effective Teachers

VESNA NIKOLIC

HANNA CABAJ

Pippin

Copyright © 2000 by Pippin Publishing Corporation
Suite 232, 85 Ellesmere Road
Toronto, Ontario
Canada M1R 4B9

Edited by Anne Fullerton
Designed by John Zehethofer
Illustrated by Pat Cupples
Typeset by Jay Tee Graphics Ltd.
Printed and bound in Canada by Friesens

We acknowledge the financial support of the Government of Canada through the Book Publishing Industry Development Program for our publishing activities.

Canadian Cataloguing in Publication Data

Nikolic, Vesna
    Am I Teaching Well?: self-evaluation strategies for effective teachers

Includes bibliographical references.
ISBN 0-88751- 087-6

1. Teachers – Self-rating of. I. Cabaj, Hanna. II. Title.

LB2838.N54 1999   371.14'4   C99-931558-7

10   9   8   7   6   5   4   3   2   1

*To our parents in Croatia and Poland, for teaching us
the value and joy of work*

Contents

Preface

As teachers, we reap the rewards of our work and actions perhaps more than do members of any other profession. By constantly exploring, re-examining, and modifying our teaching procedures and style, we can ensure that those rewards are there throughout our careers. In this book, we offer ideas and strategies to help you identify your strengths and weaknesses so that you can capitalize on the former, address the latter, and by doing so reach your full potential as a teacher.

You are most likely the reader that we had in mind while we were working on this book: a classroom practitioner hard at work "in the trenches," with a drive for self-improvement strong enough that you already think deeply about your classroom behaviors. We hope that this book will help you develop ways of focusing that thinking to achieve concrete goals. We also hope that supervisory staff, teachers in training, and teacher trainers will find this book useful. In fact, it is our wish that this book reach as many interested members of our profession as possible, and to that end, we and our publisher grant readers permission to photocopy, without infringement of copyright, any charts marked with the symbol ▯ for their own personal use.

We are both language teachers and the research we drew on while writing the book comes largely from the professional literature in that area, and especially from second-language teaching. Indeed, some of the book is directed toward language teachers and may not be applicable in your teaching context. There are, however, many principles of good teaching that apply across disciplines and programs, and we therefore believe that all classroom practitioners will find things in this book that they can use or adapt to positive effect.

Teaching can take an enormous number of forms—from early childhood education through content area instruction of older children and teens to academic or noncredit programs for adults. We designed this book with that variety in mind, and we also were sensitive to the enormous time pressures placed on members of our profession. The book is not intended to be read from cover to cover, but instead employs a modular approach: chapters and the sections within them are independent and can be explored in any sequence. Our suggestion is that you first take a look at the Contents pages to identify areas of teaching practice you particularly want to examine. Then, you may want to leaf through those chapters to get an idea of the sorts of tasks they contain and begin thinking about how they might benefit you. We recommend that you then read Chapter 1, particularly the last section on identifying strengths and weaknesses. Look critically at your own practice, analyzing and dissecting one area only. Identify the aspects of that area that you feel could be improved on, and select one that is important to you and that you truly believe is within your power to change. Then return to the appropriate chapter and complete the tasks. By beginning in this way, you will feel the immediate results of successful self-evaluation and be energized to tackle different and perhaps larger aspects of your practice. This small-scale experiment may only scratch the surface of your teaching skills, but it could mark the beginning of a new, career-long endeavor.

Each of the tasks we outline involves the ability to observe and think critically about one's own actions. This can be done solely through self-reflection or through self-reflection combined with video- or audiotaping, peer observation, or other techniques described in Chapter 1. We believe that a "combination" approach works best and are particularly strong advocates of taping, procedures for which are described in the Appendix. We also advocate a systematic approach and recommend the collection of self-evaluation data. More detailed suggestions about developing a teacher portfolio are included in Chapter 16.

If you are a novice teacher, it is likely that your interest is in the "what to teach" area, and you might find yourself drawn particularly to the book's earlier chapters. If you are an experienced instructor, you will probably be more eager to check the "how to" and "why" tasks found later on. Regardless of your particular interest, however, bear in mind that there are no areas of teaching that cannot be improved. Be ready to experiment and, if it seems appropriate, ask your learners to experiment with you. And remember: this book is for you. Like a diary, you can peruse it at your own pace and in your own way, and you can keep it entirely private if you choose.

The degree of success of the self-evaluation process depends largely on your determination to grow professionally and your willingness to assess your teaching patterns as objectively as possible. If systematic, focused reflection on your practice becomes a guiding principle of your professional life and you embrace it with enthusiasm, you are more likely to achieve your goals and reach your full potential as a teacher.

Enjoy your new endeavor!

Vesna Nikolic
Hanna Cabaj
Toronto, July 1999

Acknowledgments

This book could never have been started—much less finished—were it not for the fine educators who are our colleagues. We would like to express our appreciation for the inspiration and contributions, direct and indirect, of a number of individuals. Many thanks go to Leo Lynch for encouraging us to publish our work, and to Esther Podoliak for her brilliantly creative and constructive feedback at the initial stages. We are grateful also to Slawomir Wysokinski, who offered a hand with the section on lesson planning and helped us resolve many dilemmas. The video/audio self-evaluation package would not have been complete without Michael Galli's expert feedback and Lisa Morgan's generous participation in field testing. We would also like to thank the wonderful team of instructors and program consultants in the Toronto District Catholic School Board Adult Education Program, whose contagious enthusiasm and support inspired many of our tasks. We thoroughly enjoyed working with our editor, Anne Fullerton, and we are grateful to her for her constructive suggestions.

We also wish to acknowledge all we have learned from our own teachers and students in Canada, Croatia, and Poland, and from the authors listed in the bibliography and resource list, whose work has been a source of inspiration, insight, and ideas. In particular, we wish to acknowledge the following authors and publishers who granted us permission to reproduce material: David Nunan, Rebecca Oxford, Ruth Wajnryb, Luke Prodromou, David Mendelsohn, Marianne Celce-Murcia, Jadwiga Gurdek, *TESOL Quarterly*, *The English Teaching Forum*, and Cambridge University Press.

Finally, our deepest gratitude goes to our children, Martina and Marko Nikolic and Alexandra Cabaj, and to our husbands, Ivica Nikolic and Peter Cabaj. Martina was particularly helpful in providing us with numerous insights on teaching from a student's perspective. Our families sustained us through months of work in the evenings and on weekends, and this book is the tangible evidence of their unflagging love and support.

1. On the Road to Excellence

"Give a man a fish and he eats for a day. Teach him how to fish and he eats for a lifetime." These words are attributed to Confucius, and in expanding on them in the context of language learning, Tyacke and Mendelsohn (1986; quoted in Oxford, 1990) wrote, "But just as there are many different kinds of rods, different kinds of bait, and different fishing locations, all of which offer a variety of choices and experiences, there are different ways of learning language." All this may be true, but as we wrote in a 1998 article in *Contact*, if fishermen do not ask themselves whether they are using the right type of bait and rod and the appropriate methods and techniques for the fish they want to catch, they may have to buy fish on their way home.

Our intention with this reply to Mendelsohn and Tyacke is neither to begin a dialogue with them nor to propose an innovative self-evaluation program for fishermen. The meaning behind our response is simply that no professional can acquire the skills of a peak performer without absolute willingness constantly to assess, explore, examine, and improve one's practice.

Take a minute and try to picture this scenario, familiar to all teachers. During a lesson, one of your learners asks for clarification. What would you select as the best course of action?

- Respond only to that learner, looking at and talking to him or her alone.
- Repeat the question for everyone in class, and then address it.
- Repeat the question for everyone in class, and then ask if anyone knows the answer.
- Put off addressing the question until later, because you do not want to disrupt your lesson.

And while you are responding, where would you be standing?

- Next to the student who asked the question;
- At a position in the class where everyone can see you;
- Somewhere else.

Does it matter which of these options you choose? And do you ask yourself similar questions every day? If you do, you are one of those teachers who constantly strives to develop and improve teaching practice.

Evaluation seems to be part of human nature, part of an innate need to make judgments and express opinions. We evaluate others, formally or informally, but we also engage regularly in self-evaluation of our behavior, personal as well as professional. Evaluation is an integral part of the teaching process. We evaluate our teaching practice and programs to inform our decisions about planning and organization. Many of us also encourage learners to evaluate our teaching and offer feedback on the program, even if only informally.

Most of teachers' daily work is determined by judgments, decisions, and choices. Some of these are "macro" decisions, so crucial that they can make or break a class. Others, such as deciding on ways to answer a student's question, are related to micro teaching skills; they may not be critical, but they play a significant role in the classroom. The results of these major decisions and the fine-tuning of choices distinguish a weak, mediocre, or solid teacher from a peak performer.

Due to the fact that the quality of program delivery depends on decisions and choices, interest in self-assessment in teaching is growing. The importance and popularity of classroom research and teacher self-evaluation have increased rapidly since the 1950s. Self-evaluation is now a standard component of staff performance evaluation in most education systems.

The Whats, Hows, and Whys of Teaching

I touch the future. I teach.
CHRISTA MCAULIFFE, CHALLENGER SPACE SHUTTLE ASTRONAUT

In a 1982 paper, Donald Freeman proposes an implicit hierarchy of issues that teachers face as they move from the training to the development stage of professional growth. For novice teachers, the primary and dominant question is "What do I teach?" As teachers gain experience, the *what* question gives way to "How do I teach?" and an exploration of ways and means of working with learners. Finally, once the *whats* and *hows* cease to pose difficulties, we enter the third stage of our development and begin to ask ourselves, "Why do I teach what I teach, and why do I teach it the way I do?" In our opinion, this progression applies not only to novice teachers' journey to experience, but also to teachers with years of experience who face new teaching situations—a new program certainly, but perhaps even a new group of learners.

Let us imagine a seasoned professional with years of training and experience. She faces a new group of learners at the beginning of a new teaching session. For her, the first issue at hand is to conduct an analysis of learners' needs in an attempt to answer the question, "What do I need to teach?" While this is especially necessary in community-based, noncredit programs where learner populations are extremely varied, we believe it also applies to more stable or predictable teaching environments. As the teacher learns about her students' expectations, backgrounds, preferences, and learning styles, she will also begin to address the "How do I teach?" question. Only after she has responded to or at least revisited the *what* and *how* questions for the new teaching situation can she proceed with an analysis of "Why do I teach what I teach, and why do I teach it the way I do?"

Thus, Freeman's *what*, *how*, and *why* questions are part of a process of decision making and reflection that we engage in on an ongoing basis throughout our careers. How we go about answering these questions and mastering our craft is quite idiosyncratic. Many components of effective teaching could be identified, but there is no magic formula that works for all educators. The only thing you can always say about teaching is "That depends on a number of factors...." We all bring unique personalities, skills, preferences, and aptitudes into our classrooms, and so do our students. One teacher's most effective activity might be a weak point for another and overkill for a third. We do not all have to have the same understanding of methodology and practice.

In light of these differences, it would be absurd for us to prescribe recipes, claiming that they work equally well for every teacher in every class. Instead, we offer a variety of options. As readers work through the tasks we describe, they should consider their particular students, their teaching context, their own personality traits, and specifics of their programs—just to name a few variables.

Self-Evaluation: A Model and Some Techniques

All teachers self-evaluate, but most do so subconsciously and informally. A systematic approach to analyzing what is happening in the classroom is preferable to occasional reflection, however, and can lead to concrete ideas for improvement.

Our model for systematic self-evaluation, outlined in Figure 1, reflects the stages teachers may go through as they work with the collection of tasks in this book. Self-evaluation can involve many techniques. Those described in what follows are some common approaches, many of which are discussed in more detail later. Results can best be achieved by adopting a "combination" approach—that is, by using two or more of the techniques simultaneously—to yield deeper insight than is possible with any single technique.

Personal Reflection: Diaries or Journals

Through reflective writing in journals or diaries, teachers can express their feelings about their teaching, working environment, relationship with students, concerns, and successes. Written candidly immediately or shortly after a lesson, entries in a teaching diary present personal accounts of the teaching activities, observations, and reflections, and views of how the classroom

Figure 1
The Systematic Process of Self-Evaluation

Raising awareness:
- self-evaluation questionnaires and checklists
- professional development

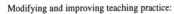

Modifying and improving teaching practice:
- writing accounts of findings
- defining goals for future development

Establishing a systematic process of self-observation:
- self-monitoring combined with video- or audiotaping or peer observation

Ensuring systematic observation and analysis of findings:
- evaluating the impact of changes in the classroom
- identifying how certain aspects of teaching practice have improved

Identifying strengths and weaknesses:
- setting priorities

Planning a course of action:
- defining criteria for evaluation of teaching behaviors
- experimenting with the identified areas of teaching

experience affects teachers' professional and personal lives. As Jack Richards suggests in *The Language Teaching Matrix*, the entries are usually analyzed for recurring patterns or salient events. The professional literature has long recognized the effectiveness of keeping a teaching diary or journal for purposes of self-evaluation. One of the most famous examples is *Teacher*, Sylvia Ashton-Warner's diary of teaching Maori children in New Zealand. First published in 1965, it is a classic in the literature on reading instruction.

Action Research: Classroom Tasks, Action Plans

Action research, a form of reflective inquiry, has been employed in professional development in education for well over forty years. It links theory and practice, providing an effective way for teachers to try out ideas in the classroom to increase their knowledge about the curriculum, teaching, and learning. A typical action research project goes through stages of reconnaissance, planning, action, observation, and reflection. It can be conducted individually or within a team, with or without learner involvement; it is based in a real situation, is highly participatory, and enables productive self-evaluation. A wide variety of examples of issues that can be explored through action research is discussed in the literature (see, for example, Jack Richards and David Nunan's *Second Language Teacher Education* or Donald Freeman's *Doing Teacher Research*).

Self-Reporting: Checklists or Questionnaires

Many teachers conduct self-evaluation through questionnaires and checklists, although no practical guide that discusses all aspects of teaching seems to exist for this approach. To some extent, we hope this book addresses this lack.

The advantage of questionnaires and checklists is that they can be answered and their findings analyzed in a nonthreatening environment. The ultimate goals of questionnaires are to raise the respondent's awareness and to promote self-observation; if this is achieved, the checklists serve their purpose well. Their shortcoming lies in the lack of objectivity of the responses—we are all prone to responding in a much more positive light than that of truth and reality.

We believe that, despite this limitation, questionnaires and checklists can be an effective component of self-evaluation if they are used in conjunction with other techniques—notably video- and audiotaping or peer observation. This involves time and commitment, but the outcomes are highly beneficial to the individual teacher and the program as a whole.

Self-Observation: Audio- or Videorecording of Lessons

Audio- or videorecording of lessons is the most reliable and accurate means of documenting what actually happens in the classroom. One way of using this procedure for self-evaluation is to record lessons for a one- or two-week period, with the goal of capturing as much class interaction as possible. One tape is then selected at random for analysis.

In *The Language Teaching Matrix*, however, Richards points out that studies have shown that merely viewing or listening to a tape does not always improve our understanding of our own teaching. Rather, a systematic and objective way of exploring the information in the recording is required, and we have advocated this approach throughout this book. The Appendix is dedicated to a discussion of procedures for conducting video and audio evaluation, and a variety of these sorts of evaluation tasks are found throughout the book, highlighted by the ▭◗.

Professional Portfolios

Professional portfolios seem to be gaining popularity as a self-evaluation technique, especially among elementary and secondary school teachers. Portfolios are collections of materials assembled to be representative of work accomplished in a particular course, with a particular group of learners, or in an entire school year. They may include lesson plans, student work samples, program goals, records of activities outside the classroom, records of courses taken, summaries of professional books and articles, notes from students or their parents, name tags from workshops or conferences, photos, videos, and so on. The portfolio contents may be reviewed with a supervisor or peer during an evaluation meeting. The process may be facilitated by a written summary of the portfolio contents. The portfolio approach is more beneficial if it is combined with some other technique. A more detailed description and various tasks related to portfolio evaluation are found in Chapter 16.

Role Reversal: Teachers as Learners

One of the most involving ways of discovering what is really happening in the world of the classroom is to experience it as a learner yourself. Numerous accounts of teachers becoming learners appear in the literature. In a 1987 article, Tim Lowe describes an experiment in which a group of teachers became learners in a part-time course in Mandarin. The language teacher, teacher-learners, and an observer all kept diaries. It was a real learning experience for all participants; sharing impressions from their diaries helped them discover that many more things were happening in the classroom than they had ever realized.

Peer Observation

To see what is happening in the classroom more clearly—particularly if access to video- or audiotaping is not available—teachers may need assistance from their colleagues. Peer observation has long been considered conducive to teacher learning, especially if the teacher observed is an experienced one and the observation is followed by conferences and analysis of findings.

Over the years, ideas for peer observation have been revised and new methods and possibilities have been developed. Observation can be conducted in pairs or groups; a second observer may be invited to class to ensure objectivity; all parties may write diary entries or fill out checklists or observation report forms to elicit all perceptions of the lesson. Whatever the form, the value of peer observation comes not only in learning gained by the observer through watching another teacher's methods, but also in follow-up sessions. It is in postobservation discussions that we draw conclusions that help improve our teaching patterns and boost our professional growth.

In general, when done systematically and seriously, peer observation is a beneficial process for all participants. Even though it may be time consuming and costly if used as a staff-development technique, it has many advantages: it is participatory, democratic, and less threatening than supervisory observation and evaluation. We feel that, if it is conducted with an experienced practitioner, it can be particularly helpful for a teacher just starting with a program or course he has never taught before. For more objective results, it may be combined with video evaluation.

Professional Development Plans

This technique is meant to facilitate systematic professional development conducted on a sessional or annual schedule. Teachers are encouraged to state objectives for professional growth in different areas of teaching at the beginning of a new session or school year and to reflect back on the results at the end of the designated period. A further explanation of the process is provided in Chapter 16.

Group Professional Development Projects

This technique involves the whole department or school working with various self-evaluation techniques together. School administrators and supervisory staff can and should do a great deal to encourage teachers to participate in such projects by presenting the idea, making any necessary schedule changes to ensure that teachers get release time for self-evaluation, facilitating workshops and sessions that clarify the techniques proposed for use, and organizing events that not all teachers can organize on their own (video or portfolio evaluation, for example). We are all certainly more motivated to engage in self-evaluation projects if our colleagues are involved, if we can create "communities of inquiry" (Wells *et al.*, 1994), and if the project can be accommodated within our busy schedules.

Self-Evaluation versus Supervisory Evaluation

Practitioners and theorists alike agree on the importance and value of self-assessment. Agreement on the need for formal supervisory evaluation, however, would probably be found to a large extent only among school administrators. Teachers commonly find traditional supervisory evaluation stressful and complain that it is not based on clearly defined criteria. They see themselves passively practicing their listening skills while supervisors try to diagnose their weaknesses and then "pour wisdom" on their programs and deliver value judgments.

Teachers often point out that no one can pass judgment on their programs without the broad understanding of their classes, students, and other factors that only they possess. Francis Hart (1987), though a supervisor himself, agrees, claiming that no outsider can fully understand what is happening during someone else's class, since it is a complex sociolinguistic event. "To observe a class is actually to observe a class being observed," Hart reports having heard someone say during a seminar. Indeed, the presence of an observer changes the classroom atmosphere and teaching situation significantly.

We often hear of teachers who are given the *option* of being formally evaluated, but are offered incentives if they agree. One can easily guess what most teachers decide, regardless of the incentives. Obviously, the strategies used for conducting teacher evaluation have to be carefully selected, and supervisors need to be sensitive to all legitimate complaints and suggestions. In an attempt to improve supervisory evaluation, many administrators now encourage teachers to combine formal and self-evaluation, regardless of how contradictory that may seem. During the formal evaluation both teacher and evaluator prepare reports, and both are kept on file. This may be one route to making teacher evaluation more user-friendly for all concerned, provided that teachers are given the opportunity to express themselves freely and to explain their vision of their teaching. One goal toward which this route would naturally lead is to the introduction of self-evaluation as a model for an entire department or school.

The Benefits of Self-Evaluation

If you do not tell the truth about yourself, you cannot tell it about other people.
VIRGINIA WOOLF, *THE MOMENT AND OTHER ESSAYS*

One of the goals of many teacher support and inservice programs is to provide teachers with instruments that direct and facilitate reflection. It is through such processes that teachers grow, that teaching moves from being pursued as a trade to become a profession. Teachers who are already "converted" do not need to be convinced of this; they know that self-evaluation is highly beneficial. As for skeptics, we hope that this list of the benefits of self-evaluation will persuade them to join the army of teachers who now engage in this process:

- Self-evaluation facilitates learning and development of self-knowledge.
- It directs professional development and career planning, with resulting increases in professional satisfaction.
- It enhances feelings of job security and opens the door to growth and promotion opportunities.
- It arms teachers with tools for raising their awareness about their teaching and identifying problem areas.
- It ensures systematic and ongoing work on improving teaching patterns.
- It helps teachers better comprehend and articulate the rationales behind classroom behaviors, activities, and events.

The benefits for programs and departments include these:

- It ensures systematic work on professional growth.
- It promotes professional development, but still allows for individual differences.
- It renders staff evaluation more collaborative and participatory.
- It ensures program quality.
- As a group project, it fosters growth in the entire department or program and enhances collegiality.
- It reduces the need for formal supervisory evaluation.

How to Identify Your Strengths and Weaknesses

Teachers self-evaluate in different ways. Each teacher has his or her own priorities for areas that need improvement; in addition, educational programs are not identical in the emphasis they place on various aspects of teaching, nor do all departments base their expectations on the same elements. Since this book attempts to present a thorough guide to self-monitoring over a range of teaching aspects, readers should select tasks related to the areas that they or their departments, programs, or schools wish to focus on.

The following tasks, however, are recommended for all readers. They provide an introduction to the process of self-evaluation and are intended to help you identify particular areas on which you might choose to concentrate.

Task 1

Conducting a systematic, critical analysis of your own classroom performance takes courage. It involves a willingness to criticize your current teaching habits and requires openness to the spirit of change. Think about your determination to improve your teaching practice and to reflect on your views with the ultimate goal of changing your teaching patterns.

1. How willing are you to start a systematic process of self-analysis, instead of undertaking only casual observation?

_____

_____

2. If you are uncertain that you are willing to embark on systematic self-evaluation, identify your reasons.

Reasons: _____

_____

_____

How legitimate are they?

_____

_____

Task 2

1. Take some time to leaf through this book and try to identify the areas of teaching practice with which you feel most comfortable and most uncomfortable. The table of contents provides a summary of the aspects of classroom practice discussed, including such areas as planning, classroom interaction, group work, student motivation, and others.

I feel most comfortable with these teaching areas: I feel least comfortable with these teaching areas:

_____   _____

_____   _____

_____   _____

_____   _____

2. As you browse through the questionnaires and tasks in this book, identify the areas in which your strengths and weaknesses lie.

These are my strengths: These are my weaknesses:

_____   _____

_____   _____

_____   _____

_____   _____

3. The weak area I would like to work on first is _____

_____

4. Other weak areas that I would like to know more about and work on are _____

_____

_____

2. Your School and Professional Community

If administrators, teachers, and students can smile in the same language, they should be able to speak the same language, too. Teachers' working environments vary greatly—from one-teacher centers with a specific instructional focus, to small schools with few staff members and an emphasis either on single or multiple disciplines, to big institutions with large faculties and a full range of programs. The nature of the contact teachers have with one another and with other education professionals is determined by a number of factors, such as the physical setting and organization of space in the workplace, teaching schedules, and teachers' personality traits and "people skills." In general, teachers benefit considerably from working in large institutions, which usually offer more opportunities for exchange of ideas and reciprocal learning. Those who work on their own often express longing for collegial contact and cooperation.

We all appreciate working in a supportive and friendly group. It is well accepted that a congenial atmosphere is one of the foundations of a healthy work environment. Sharing, partnership, good will, and friendship not only strengthen professional ties but are beneficial for well-being both in and out of the workplace. Many schools can boast exemplary staff cooperation, where teachers are on the same wavelengths and joyfully contribute to the growth of their school. In others, staff manage to coexist with politeness and form groups of compatible individuals. In still others, teachers openly express resentment and bitterness, and needling appears to be the only form of communication.

Why do some groups coexist and cooperate flawlessly while others are beset by personality and professional conflicts? Is it possible to create a team from inherently incompatible individuals? These questions reveal complicated issues that baffle many school administrators. In our experience, rearranging staff groupings and organizing agreed-upon staff transfers at the earliest opportunity are often time- and energy-saving options. However, we all have a responsibility to do our part in creating a positive atmosphere in the workplace. This chapter will help you identify the challenges of staffroom interaction and encourage you to think about what you can do to improve collaboration with your colleagues.

The Working Environment

Work is love made visible.
KAHLIL GIBRAN, *THE PROPHET*

Successful interaction within any teaching environment implies solid cooperation among colleagues. That cooperation is the basis for collective professional growth. Therefore, it is important that we occasionally reflect upon how we contribute to the atmosphere of our work environment and what we can do to improve that atmosphere as we work side by side with our colleagues.

Task 1

Responding to the following questions will help you describe the manner in which you now interact with your colleagues.

1. Do you feel constrained or supported by the context within which you work? In what ways?

_____

_____

2. How do you see your role as a member of your school or program staff?

_____

_____

3. How do you address your colleagues? Do you use first names? Do you engage in informal chats?

_____

_____

4. What initiatives have you taken to contribute to professional growth within your school or department?

_____

_____

5. How do you interact with your colleagues?

	Always				Never
	5	4	3	2	1
We socialize together.					
We collaborate.					
We support one another.					
We act to motivate and inspire one another.					
We smile when we talk together.					
We share and exchange ideas and materials.					
We try to resolve conflicts, clear up misunderstandings, and reduce tensions.					
We discuss students' needs and progress.					
I encourage team work with other staff members.					
I respond to colleagues' initiatives with acknowledgment, praise, and support.					
I participate in all school activities.					
I try not to complain.					
I avoid gossiping about supervisors, students, and colleagues.					
I do not criticize colleagues, especially less trained or experienced ones.					
I attempt to fit in.					
I dress according to generally accepted norms.					

6. From the issues mentioned in question 5, identify and analyze one that you feel is a strength and one that is a weakness. Think of some examples and reflect in terms of what you now do or could do to improve collaboration and build stronger professional relationships.

_____

_____

7. Devise an action plan to implement your ideas about improving the weaknesses you have identified.

_____

_____

_____

_____

Task 2

1. By verbalizing classroom challenges and successes, we come to a better understanding of ourselves and others. Still, many of us complain that it is difficult to share problems with colleagues, mainly because of fear of losing credibility. How do you feel about this issue?

_____

_____

2. Think about your reaction when a colleague approaches to share a problem. What do you usually do?

— I offer a solution.
— I mention that the same thing has happened to me.
— I show that I am sympathetic.
— I try to come up with suggestions and ways to help.
— Other: _____

3. When you meet colleagues in the hallway, on yard duty, at the photocopy machine, or over coffee, do you discuss what they are teaching that day and what their successes or difficulties have been? Do you feel that such sharing is beneficial? Why or why not?

_____

_____

4. Do you share materials or ideas you have come across and cannot use in your own program or class but that a colleague might be able to use?

_____

_____

5. Conduct an experiment with your colleagues. For one entire teaching day, no one should use the word _I_. Instead, ask each other _you_ questions (What do you think? How do you feel?) and practice your listening skills. As a follow-up, reflect on your findings.

_____

_____

_____

_____

Task 3

Do the following task if you work in a large school, where staff meetings are held.

1. How often do you have staff meetings? Are they held during work hours? Do you feel more are needed, or fewer? Why?

_____

_____

2. Who calls them? Who creates the agenda?

_____

_____

3. After one of the meetings, review the agenda with your colleagues and identify the issues that were discussed. How relevant or important are they?

_____

_____

4. Does the choice of issues correspond to staff needs? If not, how could this be changed? What can you do to facilitate such a change?

_____

_____

5. Do you sometimes suggest agenda items? Why or why not?

_____

_____

6. Are discussions in staff meetings brief and constructive? If not, what needs to be done?

_____

_____

7. Do you contribute to discussions? Why or why not?

_____

_____

8. What (if anything) needs to be changed about these meetings?

_____

_____

_____

_____

Task 4

Blessed are those who feel comfortable with their bosses. But regardless of whether you like and respect your immediate supervisors, you may be stuck with them for an extended period. It is crucial to your well-being that you develop positive ways of communicating with supervisors and of avoiding conflict. This can be done by

- knowing and complying with general rules and policies of the workplace (even the apparently illogical ones usually have some purpose, and fighting them is often pointless in any event);
- being on time (and apologizing if an emergency makes you late);
- doing paperwork on schedule;
- offering help at "crunch" times;
- inviting your boss to class events (he or she may not be able to attend but will appreciate being informed and included);
- being positive, especially in the face of difficulties;

- bringing up suggestions or complaints with discretion and using proper channels;
- keeping a plan and materials for a substitute teacher in case of emergency or illness.

1. If you know your supervisor personally, you may be able to list additional, specific things that could be done to improve communication with her or him. Are there things to which she or he might respond particularly well? What are they?

_____

_____

2. If your relationship with your immediate supervisor is not what you would like it to be, why is this the case? Is there anything you can do to change it?

Reasons: _____

_____

What could be done: _____

_____

3. Try to recall an incident that caused conflict between you and a supervisor or colleague. In hindsight, how do you think it could have been avoided?

_____

_____

Task 5

Our learners carry personal problems and dilemmas with them, just as much as they carry the books in their backpacks. Inevitably they bring these through the classroom door.

1. Getting to know learners' problems and dealing with them is a double-edged sword. Teachers would have to be trained psychologists to fully understand many of these problems. Besides, offering assistance can too often become a burden. On the other hand, if you know nothing about your learners' hardships, you can't assess their implications for the learning process. How do you feel about this issue?

_____

_____

2. When appropriate, try to assess the relevance of becoming familiar with learners' personal situations. Think of a learner in your class whose situation you know quite well. If you were to walk a mile in his shoes, what challenges would you face? Try to identify at least five.

Learner's name: _____

Challenge 1: _____

Challenge 2: _____

Challenge 3: _____

Challenge 4: _____

Challenge 5: _____

3. What implications do these things have for this student's learning process? Does it help that you know the student's situation?

_____

_____

4. What can you as a teacher do to help this learner?

_____

_____

5. Are you aware of the economic, family, and social realities others of your learners have to face?

_____

_____

Task 6

If you teach adults, your students may be immigrants, refugees, employed or unemployed, welfare recipients, foreign-trained professionals, members of racial or cultural minorities, or parents, and all may be facing different family and social problems. In order to better empathize with your students and support their interests, how do you keep informed of the issues they face?

— I talk to students about the challenges they are experiencing.
— I talk to colleagues.
— I listen to news reports.
— I read the newspapers.
— Other: _____

Task 7

The teaching community extends beyond the school walls. We are all aware of the many teacher education courses, professional development opportunities, publications, professional associations, and other resources that are available to us. By making use of them we contribute to a positive atmosphere for education in all contexts.

1. How do you keep in touch with the profession at large?

— I read professional newsletters, journals, or other publications.
— I go to meetings, presentations, and workshops.
— I hold membership in a professional organization.
— I subscribe to or borrow publications from professional organizations.
— I visit resource centers.
— Other: _____

2. Devise an action plan that will help you assist your students and contribute to your profession even further.

_____

_____

_____

_____

3. Your Classroom, Your Students, and You

Try to picture a classroom from the "olden days"—say, a room where a language lesson was in progress. Remember those rows of students obediently slouched over their texts, conjugating Latin verbs in unison or translating Greek? If you had asked them to say "Good-bye" in the language they were learning, they probably would not have been able to. But then, they did not really need to—learning for them was not about being able to communicate their own ideas.

Readers of this book will find no resemblance between this description and their own teaching environments. Today's programs and classrooms are intended to promote enjoyment in learning, to encourage collaboration and interaction, and to help students develop real skills they will need in real life. How you organize your physical space and the mood you create in it contribute to the success of that mission.

Your Classroom

Classrooms come in a multitude of colors, shapes, and sizes. Some were designed originally as settings for learning and teaching, with plenty of room and wall space, good ventilation, and good lighting. Quite often, however, instruction takes place in conditions quite removed from that ideal. Classes for adults, particularly, may be held in adapted offices or rooms in community centers or libraries, and in the worst-case scenario, these resemble broom closets more than classrooms. Some rooms are shared by many teachers working on staggered schedules and therefore cannot be claimed by anyone as his own. The result is bare walls and a cold, unfriendly, temporary sort of feeling. Other rooms accommodate oversize classes, and the clutter of furniture allows no possibility of rearranging desks to facilitate student interaction and mobility. Even worse, in some classrooms desks are bolted to the floor in rows ready for teacher-fronted instruction.

A teacher's wish list of what a classroom should be like would probably include the following:

- spacious and clean;
- lots of chalkboard and wall space;
- good lighting and ventilation;
- ample space for storage of instructional materials;
- windows that open, with sills for plants or displays;

- large tables (rather than small desks) for group work; and
- good climate control.

We spend so much time in our classrooms that quite often we stop noticing things that a casual visitor would immediately pick up. At one time or another, we have all had books or papers piled in inappropriate places, Christmas decorations still hanging in May, chalk dust everywhere (including on ourselves!), and faded samples of student work or obsolete posters drooping on the walls. The following tasks are intended to help you look at your classroom with fresh eyes.

Task 1

1. Use the following chart to create an objective account of what a visitor would see upon entering your classroom.

Item	What do you see?
My desk (and things on it)	
Students' desks	
Other furniture	
Storage space	
Chalkboard	
Shelves	
Floor	
Walls (and things on them)	
Other: _____ _____ _____ _____ _____	

2. Identify what you like and dislike about your classroom.

_____

_____

3. Identify all the things that frustrate you about your classroom.

_____

_____

34

4. What would you like to change? Is it within your power to change these things?

_____

_____

5. If your classroom is far removed from the ideal or if you are not allowed, for example, to re-arrange furniture or post things on the walls, how do you make the most of what is available?

_____

_____

Task 2

In many cases, you can go a long way toward shaping your teaching environment. Reflect on the appearance of your classroom in general.

1. What do you do to make your classroom a pleasant, stimulating environment?

	Always				Never
	5	4	3	2	1
I organize classroom space and seating arrangements to facilitate interaction and learning.					
I display students' work in my room and elsewhere in the school.					
I display visual aids for topics currently being explored.					
I change classroom displays regularly and keep them neat.					
I involve students in decorating the room and keeping it tidy.					
Other: _____					
_____					
_____					
_____					

2. In your case, how true is the following statement: A visitor to my classroom would probably think that it looks nice, clean, and tidy.

True ❏   Somewhat true ❏   Not true ❏

3. Are there things you could improve upon? How will you do it?

_____

_____

_____

_____

Task 3

Most teachers are expected to be in class before the start of their lessons, since advance preparation of teaching aids, materials, items on the blackboard, etc., ensures that teaching time is maximized.

1. What happens in your classroom before and during each class?

	Always				Never
	5	4	3	2	1
The chalkboard is clean before the class starts.					
Materials are ready—handouts photocopied, tapes cued, and so on.					
My desk is well organized and clean.					
I set a good example by being on time myself.					
I discuss with students the cultural customs related to being on time.					
I respect break time (everyone needs it).					
Other:					

2. If an observer were asked to give an overall evaluation of your level of preparation for instructional time, what rating would he or she give?

       5   4   3   2   1
   Excellent   Poor

3. What could you improve in this area? What is your action plan for doing so?

_____

_____

_____

_____

Seating Arrangement, Your Presence, and Eye Contact

Self-help is the best help.
AESOP, *HERCULES AND THE WAGON*

The physical classroom space can go a long way to establishing an atmosphere conducive to learning. But once your students are in the room and instruction has begun, there are other things that should be kept in mind. Different arrangements of desks promote different kinds of interaction, and the way you address your students contributes significantly to the learning environment.

Task 1

Draw and label the furniture, door(s), window(s), and chalkboard in your classroom in the box below (or create a differently shaped box if necessary).

1. Look at the seating arrangement depicted in your drawing. Are you content with it?

Yes ❏   No ❏

2. How are your students seated?

— Individually, at small desks.
— In pairs.
— Grouped around tables, facing one another.
— In a semicircle facing my desk.
— In a circle.
— In rows.
— Other: _____

3. Is the seating arrangement conducive to a variety of grouping possibilities—pair, small-group, or whole-class interaction, along with individual work? Can students see and hear one another easily?

_____

_____

4. If you do not have control over classroom seating, is there anything you could do to make the most of the existing arrangement?

_____

_____

5. If the seating arrangements can be changed, what could you do to improve them?

_____

_____

Task 2

Use the picture from the preceding task and mark on it the places you usually stand during class time—for example, "X1" would indicate where you stand most of the time, "X2" a place you stand somewhat less often, and so on. (If possible, confirm this through videorecording your class for a few days.)

1. To facilitate communication and keep students involved, do you stand at a spot where everyone can see and hear you easily? Sit in different students' seats and imagine how you would feel during class if you were those students.

_____

_____

2. Are there spots in the classroom where you stand more often than others? If yes, is there any particular reason?

_____

_____

3. Once your students start doing an activity, do you circulate?   Yes ❑   No ❑

4. Experiment with changing your usual spot(s) in the classroom. What impact does this have on class interaction and dynamics?

_____

_____

5. Devise an action plan for improving this aspect of your teaching practice.

_____

_____

_____

_____

Task 3

Analyze your classroom presence and the way you maintain eye contact. If possible, do this by watching a videorecording of yourself teaching.

1. Which students do you usually look at while talking? Where in the room do these students sit?

_____

_____

2. Do you have any specific reasons for focusing on these students and classroom positions? If so, what are they? If not, would you like to alter anything?

_____

_____

3. Do you tend to look over the students' heads? Yes ❑   No ❑

4. Do you feel that making eye contact benefits students? Yes ❑   No ❑

5. Are your students aware of the importance of eye contact in western cultures? Yes ❑   No ❑

6. Do you think that all your students feel they get a fair share of your attention?

_____

_____

7. Devise an action plan to improve this aspect of your teaching practice.

_____

_____

_____

_____

Task 4

While doing an activity with the whole class, a teacher asks one student to read aloud. As the student starts reading, the teacher moves to stand by the student's desk, anticipating that he will need help. The student begins to read more softly, concentrating on the teacher, with the result that some of his peers now cannot hear him. These students, realizing that the teacher is busy with this student, start talking among themselves. It takes the teacher quite a while to regain control of the class and to get students' attention.

1. The next time you are working on a whole-class activity and during it ask one student to read aloud, do an experiment by filling out this chart.

What do I do?	Insert a checkmark each time.	Why did I do that?
I remain in the same spot.		
I move closer.		
I stand beside the student who is reading.		

2. Do your different actions have different effects? If yes, what are they?

_____

_____

Task 5

One source of frustration in the classroom may be related to an inappropriate number of students.

1. How many students do you have in your class (or, on average, in each of your classes)?

40

2. Do you feel that the number is appropriate for the space and your obligations? If the number is high, how do you cope? If the number is low, what can you do to attract additional students?

_____

_____

3. If you have a continuous inflow of students, how do you cope?

— Do you help new students catch up with the class?
— Do you show new learners your course outline, telling them what they have missed and explaining how you might work together to cover this material?
— Do you assign a peer mentor to each new student?
— Do you teach more than one group within your class and assign the new learner to an appropriate group after assessment?
— Other: _____

4. Are you content with the way you are dealing with this situation? If not, what is your action plan?

_____

_____

_____

_____

Chalkboard Use and Organization

A teacher found an old jar in the corner of his classroom. As he picked it up, it fell out of his hands, breaking into pieces—and out came a genie (of course!) who granted the teacher three wishes. The first was for a new car. *Voilà*! Through the classroom window, the teacher saw a car waiting. His second wish was for a classroom equipped with everything that modern technology has to offer. Within seconds, he was surrounded by the latest and best equipment. "What is your third wish?" asked the genie.

The teacher looked around. "How about a chalkboard and a great big box of chalk?"

Task 1

Despite technological advances, a chalkboard is still one of the most useful and reliable teaching aids. Even in the most resource-poor programs, a board is usually available. Reflect on how you use the chalkboard by checking the appropriate column for each statement.

	Always				Never
	5	4	3	2	1
I begin with a clean board, if possible.					
I write legibly.					
I avoid mixing printing and cursive writing or upper- and lowercase letters.					
I start writing on the left-hand side.					
I keep my writing organized and neat.					
I use colored chalk.					
I erase as often as appropriate.					
I keep my back turned to the class for short periods only.					
I avoid talking while writing on the board with my back to the class.					
When I'm writing on the board, I turn around occasionally and talk about what I'm writing in order to address students who are not visually oriented.					
I ask students if they can read my writing.					
I ask students whether their perception of what needs to be written on the board matches my practice.					
I encourage students to write on the board.					
Other: _____					
_____					
_____					

Task 2

In her 1993 book *Classroom Observation Tasks* (p. 123), Ruth Wajnryb describes the board as an invaluable classroom resource and suggests the following organization of space to maximize its effectiveness:

Reference material (permanent)	Main section—developmental stages of lesson	Impromptu notes—"perishables"

1. How does this organization compare to the way you use the board?

_____

_____

2. Does this organization, along with what you learned by completing the preceding task, suggest any areas that could be improved? If so, what are they?

_____

_____

3. Create an action plan for making the improvement(s), and monitor progress for about a week. What happened?

_____

_____

_____

_____

Your Role in the Classroom

All the world's a stage.
WILLIAM SHAKESPEARE, *AS YOU LIKE IT*

Task 1

Teachers assume a number of different roles, depending on their perceptions, methodology, and preferences. In *Classroom Observation Tasks*, Ruth Wajnryb explains that the role assumed also depends on the stage of the lesson.

1. Think of yesterday's lesson. Place a checkmark next to the descriptors that best fit the roles you took on during its various stages. Then circle the roles that you would *like* to see yourself in.

manager	conductor	stimulator	psychologist
controller	checker	motivator	actor/performer
authority	monitor	helper	presenter
organizer	lecturer	facilitator	assistant
assessor	informer	provider of services	consultant
initiator	explainer	entertainer	other:

2. Most of the time you see yourself as a(n) _____

43

3. You would most like to see yourself as a(n) _____

4. How can you come to fill the role selected in question 3?

_____

_____

Task 2

In the 1995 article "Taming the Big 'I': Teacher Performance and Student Satisfaction," Jeremy Harmer discusses results of an interview conducted with a number of teachers from different countries. The primary question was "Are you a different person in the classroom than you are out of the classroom?" Many teachers responded that in the classroom they felt like performers on stage and that they exhibited more positive characteristics (humor, creativity, etc.) in class than they did in "real life."

How would you respond to the same interview question?

_____

_____

Task 3

Successful students are usually those capable of organizing the input they receive, keeping their class notes and handouts in order and referring to them on a regular basis. In order to help stu-

dents, our roles can extend beyond delivering input to showing students how that input can be managed.

1. To what extent do you feel that a well-organized student notebook or binder with different sections for different activities affects students' progress in the program?

_____

_____

2. Do any of your students carry their class handouts and papers in a disorganized, dog-eared pile? Do some of them lose their handouts or leave them behind? Do you think that your role as an organizer, controller, and helper forces you to intervene? If yes, what should you do? If no, why not?

_____

_____

3. In general, do you feel teachers should encourage students to keep well-organized notebooks and class materials? If so, how?

_____

_____

4. Do you encourage students to take down the date and objective for each lesson and to keep well-organized notes? How much control should the teacher exert in this area?

_____

_____

5. What factors influence your decisions on this aspect of teaching and learning?

_____

_____

4. Program Design

Real-estate agents say that there are three significant factors to consider when buying a house: location, location, location. If asked to name three factors essential to successful teaching, many teacher trainers would agree on preparation, preparation, preparation.

Solid preparation takes considerable effort but is important for all teachers, particularly novice ones. It involves conducting a needs analysis, defining goals of the program, creating a long-range plan, and undertaking systematic work and reflection on daily lesson plans. It results in a well-designed and -implemented course, built around goals relevant for a particular group of students and including units and topics approached through motivating activities that address students' needs and interests. Such planning gives students and teacher a clear picture of course content and organization.

Because it is so time consuming, preparation is probably the least popular and most burdensome aspect of teaching. At the same time, teachers and teacher trainers (and students!) would certainly recognize it as one of the most rewarding. The consolation is that it does become easier as years go by and a teacher's repertoire of techniques and materials grows.

With this chapter we hope to help you develop the frame of mind necessary to ponder aspects of your program on an ongoing basis. We discuss program goals and ways of achieving them, curriculum, approaches to needs analysis, and designs for long-range plans.

Needs Analysis

I am not a teacher: only a fellow traveller of whom you asked the way.
I pointed ahead—ahead of myself and ahead of you.
GEORGE BERNARD SHAW, *GETTING MARRIED*

Imagine you are having guests for dinner. Prior to deciding what to make and how to serve it, you will probably try to find out what they like and dislike, whether they have any food allergies, if they are vegetarian or keep a restricted diet. Conducting a needs analysis with a new group of students is a similar process. Instead of plunging in with a trial-and-error technique, it is essential that you find out about your students' needs, interests, expectations, preferences, and dislikes before commencing work with them. This will allow you to provide a program that is relevant, adequate, and appropriate. The process results in a course enjoyable and beneficial to your students, and also demonstrates to them from the outset your genuine interest in their needs. Such deep commitment is usually highly appreciated.

Task 1

If you frequently ask students how effectively the program is meeting their needs, they will know that you are genuinely interested in helping them achieve their goals.

1. How often do you conduct needs analyses in your program?

— At the beginning of the course only
— At the beginning of the course and whenever the composition of the class changes
— At regular intervals (monthly, weekly, etc.) throughout the course

2. Do you feel that the frequency of needs analyses ought to be adjusted?

_____

_____

3. What elements of needs analysis do you identify and take into consideration? Rank the following with numerals to indicate how much attention you pay to each, leaving a blank beside any that do not play a role in your thinking.

— Students' level of proficiency
— Students' individual learning styles
— Students' individual goals for learning
— Knowledge and skills that students will need once they finish the course
— What students should be able to do when they finish the course
— The settings in which they will use their learning
— Other: _____

4. Develop an action plan for improvement in this area.

_____

_____

_____

_____

Task 2

1. How do you conduct needs analyses? Indicate the percentage of time you use each of the following techniques.

— Surveys and questionnaires, including questions or multiple-choice statements related to all relevant aspects of the program: ____%

— Class brainstorming on topics to be covered or given priority:____%
— Small-group brainstorming on topics to be covered: ____%
— "Mind mapping" techniques in which students use drawings or pictures to illustrate their daily activities in order that their needs can be determined:____ %
— Individual interviews or conversations with students:____ %
— Picture selection (for younger or less proficient students) in which students respond to pictures representing various units and topics that could be covered:____ %
— Other: _____ %

2. Do you feel that the techniques you have used so far are appropriate for your students? Have you asked their opinion?

_____

_____

3. We all know that preferences and styles for teaching and learning are extremely varied. Have you checked if the teaching style you use is the style your students prefer?

_____

_____

4. Have you developed a checklist or questionnaire for your students related to their learning preferences and styles? Have you discussed these with your students? Have you analyzed their responses and reactions? Are they reflected in your program's statement of goals?

_____

_____

5. In *The Self-Directed Teacher*, David Nunan and Clarice Lamb offer a variety of techniques, strategies, and questionnaires that can be used when conducting needs analyses. If you have the book or can obtain it, identify the questionnaires that you find most useful. How would they need to be adapted for your students?

_____

_____

6. Based on your responses to all the questions above, do you feel you have an understanding of what your students' needs are? Summarize the results of your observations.

_____

_____

_____

_____

Program Goals

One of the steps in designing a course outline is to define a set of general goals. This will help you clarify and make concrete your thinking about the aims of the program. Goals might include

- assisting students in achieving competencies required for their pursuit of occupational or educational goals;
- helping students master a subject discipline; or
- providing students with the means to develop their communicative abilities.

Task 1

1. How are your program goals defined? Formulate a statement of goals and note it below.

_____

_____

2. Check the results of the needs analysis conducted with your current group of students. To what extent are students' needs compatible with program goals?

_____

_____

3. Did your comparison of needs and goals reveal any program strengths or weaknesses?

_____

_____

4. What changes, if any, do you need to make in the statement of goals for your program?

_____

_____

5. What implications do these changes (if any) have for your next needs analysis?

_____

_____

6. Devise an action plan for this aspect of your teaching practice.

_____

_____

_____

_____

**IT IS IMPORTANT THAT TEACHERS FEEL
COMFORTABLE WITH THE CURRICULA THEY ARE USING.**

Curricula, Course Outlines, and Long-Range Plans

In the beginning there was chaos.

Preparing to teach obviously involves knowing the course curriculum. Whether you are designing the course yourself or following a predetermined outline, you will need to consider how it
will proceed over the long term, from the first day to the day your students leave your class.

Task 1

Many teachers do not have the option of designing their own course. What circumstances do you
work in?

1. I have to follow a preset curriculum, designed by the school, department, or another agency.
Yes ❑   No ❑   Partly ❑   Selectively ❑

> If so, how do you feel about the curriculum? Did you have input into designing it? Have
> you ever provided your supervisors with feedback on it?

_____

_____

51

2. I have to design a course for each new group of students.
Yes ❑   No ❑

    If so, do you adapt an established curriculum for each new group? How?

_____

_____

3. I have to use a syllabus presented in a commercial publication instead of a curriculum.
Yes ❑   No ❑   Selectively ❑

    If so, how do you feel about the syllabus? Have you ever provided your supervisors with feedback on it?

_____

_____

Task 2

Preparing your long-range plan may include selecting the units and topics to teach, deciding on the amount of time to allot to each of them, setting lessons at the appropriate level, and so on.

1. Decisions related to your long-range plan are so crucial that they can make or break your course. Wrong decisions can lead students to develop a negative attitude about your class, thereby undermining learning, or, in the case of adult learners, drive them away in search of a better-planned program. Which decisions do you feel are particularly important? List and rank them below.

	Essential				Less important
Decisions related to . . .	5	4	3	2	1
_____					
_____					
_____					
_____					
_____					
_____					
_____					
_____					

2. Analyze your long-range plan. Which of the following is it based on?

Goals	Functions	Structures
Objectives	Units and topics	Resources
Outcomes	Tasks	Skills

3. What determined the choices you made in designing your long-range plan?

_____

_____

4. Does your long-range plan include a balance of components?

_____

_____

5. Do you feel that the balance is appropriate for your group of students?

_____

_____

Task 3

Now look at your long-range plan or course outline and determine if you have identified the subject matter, topics, units, structures, skills, and so on that you plan to teach. Have you sequenced the components logically? Do you spiral course content and topics, coming back to review and expand on material previously taught? Have you designed appropriate activities?

1. If a colleague read your long-range plan, would she be able to identify what your students will be able to do at the end of your course?
Yes ❑   Partly ❑   No ❑   I don't know ❑

2. Ask a colleague to read your course outline. Is your response to question 1 correct?
Yes ❑   No ❑

3. Answer these questions about your long-range planning practice.

In order to develop a solid long-range plan...	Always	Usually	Sometimes	Never
I base it on my students' level of proficiency, needs, goals, and interests, as identified through a needs analysis.				
I create a clear and appropriate course outline and make it available to students.				
I ask for students' suggestions on units and topics.				

In order to develop a solid long-range plan...	Always	Usually	Sometimes	Never
I sequence units and techniques from "easier" to "more difficult".				
I take into account the development of all the skills included.				
I reflect on and improve my long-range plan over time.				
I show sensitivity to the developmental stage of my students and to their personal situations.				
I include events in the community in my program.				
I include sociolinguistic aspects of language.				
Other: _____				

4. Based on an analysis of your answers, what areas of planning may require work over the next few weeks? What is your action plan?

_____

_____

_____

_____

Planning for Task-Based Instruction

Your long-range plan will include many aspects of what will be taught, why, when, and how. The "how" component clearly relates to the overall philosophy of instruction in your program. Many programs today follow a task-based instructional approach—that is, rather than the teacher delivering the course content through lectures and traditional assignments, students pursue learning through a series of hands-on activities. By opting for such an approach, teachers ensure that their students are equipped with real-life skills they will need outside the classroom.

Task 1

In a presentation at a 1996 conference of the Teachers of English to Speakers of Other Languages (TESOL), David Nunan and Rebecca Oxford identified the following features of a task-based language-teaching program. Read the list below and check the items that apply to your program. Does or will your program include

- Clear instructional goals
- Authentic/naturalistic data

- Cooperative group tasks
- Linked sequences of tasks
- Models/examples of what is expected
- Functional approach to grammar
- Opportunities for learners to make choices
- Opportunities for active, creative use of language
- Opportunities for students to contribute their own ideas, opinions and feelings
- Opportunities for students to self-check and self-assess
- Outside-class application opportunities

Task 2

While designing tasks to be carried out in class, it is important to keep in mind students' lives outside the classroom. By doing so, we ensure that our task-based programs provide students with the language and skills they require to perform real-world activities and to meet real-world needs. The selection and development of those tasks is entirely determined by needs analysis.

Nunan (1989, p. 40) makes a distinction between *pedagogic tasks* and *real-world tasks*. The former "require learners to do things which it is extremely unlikely they would be called upon to do outside the classroom." Such tasks might include asking students to answer questions based on a contrived reading excerpt or staged conversation, or to decide which statements are true or false. Obviously, a certain number of such tasks will be a necessary part of any program, but they are most effective if they have clear links to life outside the classroom. Real-world tasks, on the other hand, "require learners to approximate, in class, the sorts of behaviors required of them in the world beyond the classroom." An example might be having students listen to a radio talk show and discuss whether they agree or disagree with a caller.

Randall Lund (1990) suggests that all tasks in the classroom start as pedagogic but eventually resemble real-world ones more and more. Even though real-world and pedagogic tasks cannot always be clearly distinguished, it is important that teachers make a conscious effort to incorporate both.

1. Examine some recent lesson plans, identify the tasks they include, and then fill in the chart below. The first row gives an example.

Pedagogic tasks	Real-world tasks	Tasks in column 1 prepared students for these real-world tasks
To develop listening comprehension, students listen to a tape- recorded traffic report and place checkmarks next to statements about it that are true.	*Students receive a list of locations mentioned in a tape-recorded traffic report. Prior to listening, they select a location where they will be "driving." During playback of the tape, they determine whether their location is affected by adverse traffic conditions and decide how this might affect their chosen route.*	*Students need to be able to comprehend traffic reports so they can make quick decisions about route changes.*
1. _____ 2. _____ 3. _____	1. _____ 2. _____ 3. _____	1. _____ 2. _____ 3. _____

2. Were you able to determine how the pedagogic tasks conducted in your classroom have prepared your students for something in the real world? If not, how could you redesign these tasks?

_____

_____

_____

_____

Task 3

Select and evaluate one of the tasks you expected students to perform in the past few days. Consider first whether it was pedagogic or real world, and then complete the following chart.

	Very much so			Not at all	
	5	4	3	2	1
The task was set at the appropriate level for all or most students. (If not, think about how it could be modified.)					
The task was interesting and motivating enough to keep students involved.					
I structured the task to involve real-world types of communication.					
The task was based on students sharing information, which thereby created a real need for cooperation and communication.					
I designed the task differently from others used on that day or during that week, to provide variety.					
It was designed to prepare students for vital tasks in the out-of-classroom world.					

Task 4

In many instructional settings, teachers must follow a prescribed curriculum in which pedagogic tasks are emphasized. This is often the case in high school ESL classes, for example, where teachers are involved in providing recent immigrants with the language they need to cope with other school subjects. If this is your situation, there are still things you can do to ensure that the pedagogic tasks you must use are meaningful.

1. List several common tasks in your program and evaluate the degree to which they assist students in achieving overall goals.

Task: _____

        5   4   3   2   1
Very helpful   Could be more helpful

Task: _____

     5   4   3   2   1
Very helpful   Could be more helpful

Task: _____

     5   4   3   2   1
Very helpful   Could be more helpful

Task: _____

     5   4   3   2   1
Very helpful   Could be more helpful

2. How could you modify those tasks you rated at the bottom of the scale so that they would draw connections to real-world needs and interests?

_____

_____

_____

_____

Task 5

1. If you were designing a course or program, in which order would you do the following steps? Write the numbers 1 to 4 beside the steps.

— Selecting and sequencing pedagogic and real-world tasks and activities for the classroom
— Defining program goals
— Conducting needs analyses
— Selecting and sequencing the course content

2. Describe the process of developing a task-based course, drawing on the results of a needs analysis, particular program goals, content items, and real-world and pedagogic tasks.

_____

_____

_____

_____

5. Daily Lesson Planning

Lesson plans are the tools we use to reflect on content, context, techniques, materials, sequencing and timing, and a variety of other aspects of program design. They allow us to maintain the high quality of our teaching. The differences between a well-planned and an unplanned lesson are comparable to those between a movie with a script and one without. If they don't know their lines, the actors may end up shooting the good guys instead of the bad. The consequences in the classroom are not so drastic, but they definitely have a negative impact on the quality of learning and teaching.

Expectations related to daily planning vary considerably from school to school and program to program. In some contexts, teachers are expected to have long-range and daily plans and to submit them to supervisors. In others, planning is left totally to the teacher's discretion. But regardless of whether lesson planning is supervised or not, we must still think of it as a requirement. Lessons simply cannot be meaningful if they are not thoroughly prepared. Well-planned lessons flow smoothly, building on what has happened before, leading to what will happen next, and with components and segments seeming just to fall into place. They are clean, logical, easy to carry out, and—perhaps most important—they are constructed to work for your particular students.

Everyone who has seen a well-planned lesson unfold would admit that it was a pleasure to observe and participate in. Of course, we have all entered our classrooms under-prepared on occasion, and have put lessons together as we went along. Sometimes, for example, we might have a list of activities to be undertaken but no clearly defined framework for connecting them; at worst, we may have only a vague idea of what to do during the lesson. Students are smart consumers of services, and they can tell when their teacher is unprepared. Observing an improvised lesson is like watching a disaster unfold: there are all kinds of unplanned events, behavior problems, activities that drag on, and discussions that lead nowhere.

One way of highlighting for yourself the difference between a prepared and an unprepared lesson is to do the following experiment. The next time you, for whatever reason, have to teach a lesson without much (if any) preparation, write a lesson plan *after* the session, and compare this plan of what could have been done to what actually happened. An even more objective procedure is to videotape an unplanned lesson and then to analyze what went on and consider how certain events could have been avoided by planning.

The essential role of lesson planning is beyond debate. We are in a powerful position in the classroom, and we have to bear in mind that the fate of the course often depends on how thoroughly prepared we are. In this chapter teachers have the opportunity to analyze their planning practice and re-evaluate their beliefs, habits, preconceptions, and procedures.

Unit Planning

Lessons are not isolated entities but are part of a larger, longer context. Whether that context is called a unit, theme, or some other name, it indicates a sequence of lessons connected by general objectives and topic. The first step in lesson planning, then, could be thought of as unit planning. This usually involves applying a common-sense approach to selecting and sequencing components. The main question to ponder is "What knowledge and skills related to this particular area do my students lack?" In the context of second- or foreign-language teaching, the pertinent question is "What language and content related to this particular topic do my students lack for purposes of real-world communication?"

Imagine, for example, that you are a language teacher in a course whose curriculum includes study of health issues. You might begin your planning process by identifying health subtopics and related language that students would need to be able to communicate health problems or ideas in a real-world setting. The number of topics you can pursue depends on the time available for this unit in the course, while the selection of particular topics might be guided by the language content you want to teach. An ESL/EFL unit on health for a "high beginner" level, then, might contain lessons on all or some of these topics, with each linking to what came before and will come after:

- identifying health problems;
- describing symptoms;
- making and following suggestions related to health problems;
- home remedies;
- making or canceling a doctor's appointment;
- visiting the doctor, describing symptoms, and following directions;
- a visit to a pharmacy, prescription and nonprescription drugs; and
- a visit to a medical specialist or dentist.

After deciding on lesson topics, you would analyze the general objectives for the unit, consider the tasks students have to perform outside the classroom, and build a list of language components—structures, functions, vocabulary, pronunciation, and other skills—that need to be taught and could fit into the topics. For example, if the topic is a visit to the pharmacy, you could design lessons after pondering answers to these questions:

- What language tasks do people carry out in that context?
- What language do people use when talking about medications, their effects, and their side-effects?
- What language will students need to ask for advice about medications?

Task 1

Do you plan around units? If so, analyze two of them.

1. How do they correspond to the needs analysis you conducted for your class?

_____

_____

2. How do lessons in the units reflect real-world situations your students will face?

_____

_____

3. How do particular components of your units and the skills and knowledge they aim to teach reflect the general objectives?

_____

_____

4. How well are the lessons within your unit linked so that they build on and reinforce one another? How could you improve this aspect of the unit?

_____

_____

The Process of Designing a Lesson Plan

No lesson plan will work equally well for all groups of students. Our purpose with this section, therefore, is not to prescribe a format for lesson planning but to walk through an example of the process in order to outline the important factors and some common errors.

Lesson plans can take many different forms and include a wide variety of content. The lesson planning process that follows illustrates a simple, generalized version of the sort of plan that could be created to achieve the described objectives. Individual teachers could add more versatility or more local context to the planning, develop new activities, or rely more on published materials. If you are a novice teacher, read this section to get an idea of possible routes on the lesson-planning journey and the choices you might face along the way. Experienced teachers may choose to compare the plan outlined here with their own model, in order to focus reflection and identify areas for improvement.

Imagine the following situation. Bob teaches ESL to a group of 25 immigrants to an English-speaking country. His students are adults of different ages and educational and cultural backgrounds. They need language to survive and thrive in their new environment, and they want to improve their communication skills as quickly as possible. Overall, they are at a high beginner level of English proficiency. What process does Bob go through when planning a lesson?

The Initial Assessment: Asking "What" Questions

Bob's first step in creating a lesson plan is to determine the content that needs to be taught. A needs assessment conducted at the beginning of the program indicated his students' desire to learn language to cope with problems and emergencies. Bob is teaching a unit on health and has decided that the objective for today's lesson is to enable his students to communicate health problems to a doctor. Bob wants to empower the students with strategies, structures, and vocabulary and then applaud as they produce the language they would need in such a situation during a communicative task staged as the lesson's grand finale. The first part of Bob's lesson plan might look like this:

> *Date:* January 18
> *Duration:* 5 hours
> *Unit:* Health
> *Topic:* Health problems/A visit to the doctor
> *Objective:* Students will be able to describe/explain their health problems to their doctors and obtain and understand medical advice

One of the most common traps of the lesson-planning process is to start brainstorming a list of activities and materials that could be used without considering seriously the desired objectives. The result is usually a mismatch between objectives and activities. Although starting the process by listing activities is by no means an incorrect method, teachers who decide on this course need to be careful not to lose touch with lesson and unit objectives.

With an objective defined, Bob now asks himself, "What language components will my students need to describe and explain their health problems to a doctor? What vocabulary and expressions do I need to preteach for students to be able to achieve the objective I've identified?" Bob knows his students' vocabulary proficiency well enough that he can identify words and expressions they may be lacking. He then asks, "What grammatical structures are related to the topic?" Bob's lesson plan may now look like this:

> *Vocabulary:* headache, ear ache, pain, stomach ache, broken/sprained; review names of body parts
> *Structures:* present perfect tense with since and for (describing duration of illness)
> *Language function:* asking for/giving advice
> *Pronunciation:* stress in compound nouns (e.g., headache)

62

Options for Answering the "How to" Questions

Once the what-to-teach questions have been answered, the relevant question becomes how to teach the content. Generally, the sequence of the lesson should follow the natural sequence of learning. Some teachers will recognize this as the "three *P*s" approach of presentation, practice, and production; others will recognize this as *precommunicative practice* followed by *communicative practice*. First the new knowledge, skills, topic, information—or whatever the "what" of the lesson—is presented or taught. Then learners are given a chance to try things out, make mistakes, receive feedback, be corrected, and try again. Finally, they have opportunities to use the newly learned concepts on their own.

For Bob, the first choice is between two broad possibilities for introducing new content. His decision will depend on learner preferences, expectations, and learning and teaching styles, and it will feed into his decisions about the nature and sequencing of the lesson's other activities. Both approaches have strengths and weaknesses, and they should both be part of the teacher's repertoire, in order to provide balance and avoid dull routine.

In a *deductive presentation*, movement is from the larger context to the building blocks. This is a discovery technique, and in Bob's teaching context it might involve a listening activity with a patient-doctor dialogue intended to activate the students' knowledge, build and expand on it, and help students discover how the language works. This type of introduction would be followed by practice activities moving from more to less controlled and culminating in the communicative task.

An *inductive presentation* starts with the building blocks. For Bob this would mean directed preteaching of vocabulary and structures followed by vocabulary, structures, and practice activities, and, finally, a role-play.

Bob's lesson plan may now include a description of the procedures he intends to use:

1. Warm-up and review. Start with small talk, then review yesterday's lesson and the homework. Announce the topic of the day.

2. Presentation/Introduction: Option A. Play a patient-doctor dialogue several times. With each playback, ask more detailed questions or pose a more complex task. In the process, teacher guides the students to discover new structures, vocabulary, and their use.

Option B. Ask: What kind of health problems do people have? Students brainstorm in small groups, create a list of problems and doctor's suggestions, and write them on the board. Discuss responses with the whole class; correct spelling errors, etc., together, and fill in some blanks if needed.

3. Practice. Start with a matching activity—health problems to be matched with possible remedies. Answers taken up with the whole class. Review present perfect tense; explain "since" and "for." Create a topic-based grammar exercise focusing on since and for or do related exercises from the grammar book. Talk about and practice some specific expressions people use to obtain medical advice and help.

4. Production. Class brainstorming—work with whole class to reconstruct a "real" patient-doctor dialogue; write it on the board. Students pair off. Assign roles—half are patients with a variety of health problems, half are doctors. "Patients" communicate their medical problems to "doctors," who give "medical advice." When they are finished, students change partners to get a "second opinion" from a different doctor.

5. Feedback and follow-up. Move around among the pairs; note any common problems and follow-up with whole class after second dialogues are completed. Ask if they want to try a third dialogue.

Evaluation: Asking why

The last stage of designing a lesson plan is to evaluate the activities against the intended objectives and desired outcomes. A well-planned lesson is not a motley collection of activities but a sequence organized for a purpose.

Task 1

1. Analyze Bob's lesson plan. Is the objective—students will develop the ability to communicate their health problems to a doctor—achievable through the set of activities outlined?

Yes ❑   No ❑   To some extent ❑

2. Does each of the activities play a part in achieving the overall objective? If yes, how? If no, why not?

_____

_____

3. How does this lesson plan relate to your teaching circumstances? Would something similar be feasible with your learners? What might hinder its realization in your class(es)? What, if anything, would you like to change in it?

_____

_____

_____

_____

4. How does Bob's lesson planning process differ from your own?

_____

_____

_____

_____

Task 2

A group of students is leaving the classroom after a lesson. A visitor stops them and asks, "What did you study today?" "English," they respond unanimously after an awkward pause.

Think about your students. Would they be able to provide a more specific answer in the same situation? Find out by asking students this question after your next class.

_____

_____

Task 3

The professional literature contains numerous accounts of teachers taking courses because of their desire to experience the teaching process from the learners' perspective. In the 1991 *ELT Journal* article "The Myth of Learner-Centredness; Or the Importance of Doing Ordinary Things Well," O'Neill describes an experienced language teacher who decided to take a Spanish course and found out first hand what it was like to be an adult language learner. He commented that he benefited most from lessons that were clearly formatted and organized, with well-articulated transitions between stages. (He mentioned also that these lessons were quite different from his own!)

Have you been involved as an adult learner? If so, how did you feel as a learner, and how did this affect your own teaching? If not, how do you think you would feel?

_____

_____

Lesson Objectives

In "What's an Objective Anyway?," an aptly titled article in *TESL Canada Journal*, Janet Eyring defines lesson objectives as learning outcomes that result from classroom instruction. Objectives state what students will be able to do at the end of the lesson and reflect the extent to which we expect that teaching will result in learning. Defining objectives well—and, above all, accomplishing them—is one of our essential tasks.

When working on planning, teachers usually pay more attention to a lesson's content, activities, and stages than to assessing how each lesson segment fits into objectives. But determining what learners will be able to do as a result of instruction deserves as much attention as identifying what will be taught and how.

Task 1

Reflect on the importance of objectives in your lesson plans.

1. How important do you feel defining objectives is in the lesson-planning process?

```
        5   4   3   2   1
Very important      Not important
```

2. Do you feel you devote enough time to defining objectives?

Yes ❑   No ❑   Probably ❑

3. When you finish writing your lesson plans, do you go back to check whether the activities you selected will actually help learners accomplish the identified objectives?

Yes ❑   No ❑

4. What do you do if the objectives and the activities do not match?

—I redefine the objectives.
—I change or adjust the activities.
—Other: _____

5. If objectives are intended to describe the result of classroom instruction, then well-formulated objectives should be specific and expressed in terms of observable and measurable behaviors. Such a formulation might state that students will be able to "list", "compare and contrast", "report", "explain", or "describe", rather than "know", "understand," or "learn." Further, objectives should not describe what students will be doing during the actual lesson (e.g., "read a story," "study the vocabulary") but rather what they will be able to do as a result of your instruction. Read the following examples of objectives and reflect on how their formulation differs from yours.

- Students will be able to write about a past event.
- Students will be able to describe a typical day in their own or someone else's life.
- Students will be able to call directory assistance and obtain the phone numbers they need.
- Students will be able to identify various means of transportation and talk about the transportation they use.
- Students will be able to write a note to the teacher explaining a child's absence from school.

6. Leaf through your lesson plans and make a list of the verbs you use to define objectives. Do they all express "observable", "measurable" behaviors?

_____

_____

Task 2

Analyze the way your objectives are worded.

1. Are they clear and understandable?
Yes ❑ No ❑ Almost ❑

2. Do they define what learners will be able to do at the end of—rather than during—the lesson?
Yes ❑ No ❑ Almost ❑

3. Are there sufficient objectives for each lesson?
Yes ❑ No ❑ Almost ❑

4. Do you manage to accomplish the objectives without rushing?
Yes ❑ No ❑ Almost ❑

5. Do you provide sufficient opportunity for practice before expecting students to attain each objective?

Yes ❑ No ❑ Almost ❑

Task 3

Good lesson planning is not easy. Potential problem areas related to objectives include

- lack of a clear definition;
- defining the objectives well, but overlooking them during the lesson so that things take an unexpected turn in the classroom;
- existence of a mismatch between students' and teacher's perceptions of the objectives;
- existence of a conflict between students' and teacher's perceptions of the objectives.

In general, difficulties related to defining objectives, organizing lessons so that they can be achieved, and explaining them to students diminish with experience. Beginning teachers may devote more time to the "what" and "how" elements of the lesson than to the "why." To avoid such difficulties, try the following task.

1. Before three of your next lessons, fill out the objectives column in the following chart. At the end of each lesson, ask your learners for feedback on what they thought the objectives of the day were. (Make sure your learners understand the word *objectives*.) Now complete the chart. What conclusions can you draw?

	The objectives I set	What learners thought the objectives were	Digressions I made in class: Why? Were they justified?
Lesson 1			
Lesson 2			
Lesson 3			

2. Is there considerable difference between the objectives you set and those perceived by your students? If so, devise an action plan to address this issue.

_____

_____

_____

_____

Transitions

A well-planned lesson has clearly defined stages with smooth transitions from one to the next. Its framework might look like this:

Clearly signaled beginning
↓
Statement of objectives
↓
Explanation of lesson procedures and activities
↓
Body (segments each with a clear purpose, linked sequentially and to the objectives)
↓
Conclusion (summary, clearly signaled ending)

Task 1

Analyze the framework of a recent lesson plan against the one above.

1. How did you start your lesson?

_____

_____

2. How many lesson stages can you identify?

_____

_____

3. How were the stages related to one another?

_____

_____

4. How were they related to the objectives?

_____

_____

5. How did you signal transitions from one stage to the next?

_____

_____

6. Was there a logical connection between the stages?

_____

_____

7. How did you end the lesson?

_____

_____

8. What can you conclude?

_____

_____

Task 2

Before you teach your next lesson, identify at least two of its stages and think about what you are going to say or do to link them.

The stages	The transition
1.	
2.	
Others:	

After the lesson, think about whether the planned transition worked out well.

_____

_____

Finding Variety in the Routine

Is not life a hundred times too short for us to bore ourselves?
FRIEDRICH WILHELM NIETZSCHE, *BEYOND GOOD AND EVIL*

Have you ever tried to identify the ingredients of an uninteresting lesson? The list would probably include repetition of the same sorts of activities in the same order, reusing the same resources, and lack of variety in topics. A common misconception among teachers (especially teachers of adults) is that using the same format and approach for every lesson is beneficial. Teachers sometimes say that this is what their students want, that they appreciate the familiar structure. There is, indeed, something to be said for the comfort that comes from familiar routines: the students feel informed, they prepare themselves for particular activities, and any confusion about new content is not compounded by confusion about lesson procedures. However, there is a clear line between familiarity and monotony. It is the same line that distinguishes excellence from mediocrity, creativity from dullness, sensitivity from the lack of it. Simply put, too much of any routine leads to boredom, a major classroom enemy that results in dissatisfaction, lower motivation, and profound negative effects on teaching and learning.

This is not to say that we must be wildly creative and dynamic all the time. We all remember teachers who did not bring much variety, creativity, or fun into their classes, but were still well liked and respected. Such teachers know that a teaching-matches-learning formula can make up for a certain lack of fun. But regardless of your style, hard work is required to bring the right balance of routine, variety, and excitement to your classroom.

Task 1

Think about the routines you use in teaching and the variety you build into your lessons.

1. Do you tend to use the same or similar layouts for lessons each day? Why or why not?

_____

_____

2. If you do tend to revisit the same routines, how do you avoid monotony and boredom?

_____

_____

3. Try an experiment. Teach a lesson one day using a different approach and change your routine. Involve your students: explain to them what you want to do and why, and collect feedback from them. What happened?

_____

_____

Localizing and Personalizing the Context and Content

Learning is enhanced when content and context are personalized and localized. Language learners, for example, often discover that "attaching" new vocabulary, phrases, or idioms to themselves and their own lives helps make the new language more meaningful, and therefore easier to learn and retain. Teachers should therefore avoid "clinical," dry, decontextualized content; instead, lessons should be related to people, places, and things in the learners' daily experience. For language teachers this is particularly important since these real-world connections contribute to students' processes of acculturation and settlement.

Task 1

If you are a second- or foreign-language learner yourself, try to experiment with memorizing phrases or idioms from your new language without benefit of much context. Now try attaching some others to your own "context." What happens?

_____

_____

Task 2

Analyze your last two lesson plans and respond to the questions below.

1. How did you bring your learners' personal experiences into the content of the lesson?

Lesson 1: _____

_____

Lesson 2: _____

_____

2. What current events did you draw on (if this is relevant in your teaching circumstances)?

Lesson 1: _____

_____

Lesson 2: _____

_____

3. What local issues, places, or people did you include or refer to (if this is relevant in your teaching circumstances)?

Lesson 1: _____

_____

Lesson 2: _____

_____

Keeping Your Students Informed

Task 1

1. Do you feel it is important to inform students at the beginning of each lesson about what you plan to do and what objectives you have set? Why or why not?

_____

_____

2. Does informing students about plans for the next day or few days work as a motivator? Why or why not?

_____

_____

3. Monitor how you keep your students informed by completing the following chart. For one week of teaching, place a checkmark under the days that you do the things described.

	Monday	Tuesday	Wednesday	Thursday	Friday	Saturday
I explained clearly to my students what I planned to do during the lesson.						
I explained to my students the objectives of the lesson.						
I informed my students at the end of the lesson about the lesson plan for the next day.						

4. How do your students feel? Make them more involved in the program by asking them to rate the importance they attach to being informed.

    5   4   3   2   1
Very important   Not important

5. Do you write an outline of the lesson on the chalkboard before class each day? Why or why not? Have you asked your students if they would appreciate such an outline?

_____

_____

Reflective Lesson Plans

A lesson plan is, first and foremost, a tool. It helps us keep lessons on track from the objectives to their accomplishment. But regardless of how well prepared we might be, lessons often do not proceed according to plan. As the classroom events unfold, an observant teacher might realize that things are not following the script, and adaptations and digressions might be made on the spur of the moment.

Truly effective lesson plans include notes about any changes, jotted down during the lesson for later consideration. "Went well," "Too challenging," "Took much more time than planned," "Do this after the explanation phase," and so on testify to the fact that planning is ongoing. Such notes promote reflection about teaching practice and guide us as we develop plans for future lessons.

In a 1995 article entitled "Using Lesson Plans as a Means of Reflection," Belinda Ho provides some practical advice on how to turn your everyday lesson plans into reflective ones. She suggests writing plans on the left-hand side of the page, reserving the right-hand side for reflective notes. She also advises that any digressions from the original plan be noted briefly as they occur.

Task 1

1. Follow Ho's suggestion for one lesson. Was it useful? In what ways?

_____

_____

2. At the end of each teaching day, set aside ten minutes for personal reflection. Jot down your thoughts. How do you feel the lesson went? Did everything fall into place? If not, what could have been done differently?

_____

_____

Planning Homework

Daily homework gives students additional time for learning. However, the approach to homework differs considerably across schools and programs: some include it as part of course requirements, while in others, for a wide variety of reasons, it may be totally absent.

Task 1

Consider the questions below and determine a plan of action that will ensure homework assignments in your course are carefully designed to benefit students.

1. Is homework part of your program? If not, why?

_____

_____

2. What do you see as the purpose of homework assignments?

_____

_____

3. Do your students want homework assignments? Do they enjoy them and consider them necessary?

Yes ❑   To some extent ❑   No ❑   I don't know ❑

4. If homework is a part of your program, how often do you assign it?

Daily ❑   Every other day ❑   Twice a week ❑   Once a week ❑

5. How much time do you spend planning homework assignments?

_____

6. How do you take up homework in class? Do you have students share their assignments?

_____

_____

7. Do you mark students' homework? Why or why not? If assignments are marked, how do you go about it?

_____

_____

8. What types of homework and assignments do you give?

workbook-type exercises   presentations
puzzles and games   out-of-class (community) tasks
guided writing   other
free writing

9. What, if anything, is your students' favorite type of homework?

_____

_____

Task 2

Analyze your last homework assignment.

1. What was your objective in assigning the task?

_____

_____

2. Did students have sufficient knowledge and adequate strategies to complete the homework? If not, did you help them in a lesson preceding the assignment?

_____

_____

3. How did the homework help them improve their skills?

_____

_____

4. Based on your responses to the questions above, how would you rate this particular assignment?

   5   4   3   2   1
Excellent   Poor

5. If you rated the assignment at the low end of the scale, how could you change it for a future group of students?

_____

_____

6. Is there room for improvement in this area? If yes, what is your action plan?

_____

_____

_____

_____

Overall Evaluation of Your Daily Lessons

*It is not a sign of weakness, but a sign of maturity, to rise to the
level of self-criticism.*

MARTIN LUTHER KING, JR., *WHERE DO WE GO FROM HERE?*

Looking back at your lesson plans is one way of improving your planning process. It will also help you ensure that you are covering the course outline as a whole.

Task 1

Reflect on your daily plans for the last week.

	Always	Usually	Sometimes	Never
I planned around the intended objective.				
I planned challenging, but not overwhelming, tasks.				
I included a variety of teaching strategies to address different learning styles and provide variety.				
I referred to my plan during the lessons.				
I noted changes made during the lessons.				

Task 2

Now look more closely at your last three lesson plans.

1. Is the objective of each lesson clearly stipulated in terms of what learners will be able to do at its conclusion?

Yes ❑   No ❑

2. Do your lessons follow a clear, logical framework?

Yes ❑   No ❑

3. Do the activities lead from the statement of an objective to its achievement?

Yes ❑   No ❑

4. Are the activities well sequenced?

Yes ❑   No ❑

5. Do you use a variety of material relevant to your learners?

Yes ❑ No ❑

6. Were learners provided with opportunities for practice of new skills and knowledge?

Yes ❑ No ❑

7. Did you ask yourself at the end of each lesson how well the objectives had been accomplished?

Yes ❑ No ❑

8. How true of your last three lesson plans is the following statement: "My lesson plans are so clear that a visitor to my class could identify exactly what has been taught and how by analyzing them."

_____

Task 3

This task refers to the evaluation of a single lesson. It can be undertaken as often as you wish, preferably immediately or shortly after the lesson.

1. Rate how well prepared you were for the lesson. Circle your choice.

Very well   Reasonably well   Not well enough   Minimally

2. Did the lesson flow as you planned?

_____

_____

3. Which parts of the lesson were most successful? Why?

_____

_____

4. Which parts of the lesson were least successful? Why?

_____

_____

5. What kind of teacher-student interaction occurred? How did you ensure that the students were actively involved?

_____

_____

6. How did you respond to individual needs?

_____

_____

7. How did you gain feedback from your students on the lesson?

_____

_____

8. What did you like about the lesson?

_____

_____

9. What do you think could have been done better?

_____

_____

10. Did you depart from your lesson plan? If so, did the change improve the lesson? How?

_____

_____

11. How would you teach this lesson differently next time?

_____

_____

12. How do you think it would have affected learning if the lesson had been taught differently?

_____

_____

13. How do you think students felt about this session? Did you notice any signals during the lesson that indicated how they felt?

_____

_____

14. What do you think an observer would think about this class?

_____

_____

Task 4

1. Analyze the timing of your last lesson.

	Yes				No
	5	4	3	2	1
I accomplished the objectives within the determined time frame.					
I finished all the planned activities. (If not, did you still accomplish the objectives?)					
Some students finished activities well ahead of others. (If so, how well did you deal with that?)					
I responded effectively to different students' needs in terms of timing.					

2. Is there room for improvement? If so, what is your action plan?

_____

_____

_____

_____

6. Resources

In resource-rich programs teachers have at their disposal a wide array of commercial textbooks, student workbooks, teacher reference material, audio and video aids, and an abundance of authentic materials such as magazines, newspapers, and brochures. Teachers and students may also have access to computers at school or at home. Word-processing allows teachers to create their own, very professional and easily adaptable teaching materials, and there are numerous instructional software packages and helpful sites on the Internet that add a resource dimension to just about any course or program.

In contrast, in some programs the only available teaching tool is the chalkboard, perhaps coupled with one or two copies of a textbook. Practitioners who teach or have taught in the Third World are prepared to find a heart-breaking lack of resources, but even in the "developed" world supplies vary considerably from program to program. In these settings, teachers' imaginations certainly become the most important resource of all.

Regardless of what resources are available, creativity and resourcefulness seem to be among the most useful qualities teachers can possess. Even in programs that rely on a single course textbook, we must use knowledge of the theory and practice of learning and teaching, understanding of our particular students, and creativity to provide the best possible learning experience. The security provided by a single text, with its ready-made lesson plans and familiar activities, soon gives way to boredom and reduced learning if it is not supplemented with other materials. Making the most of what we have available and using it with enthusiasm is the rule of thumb in any teaching environment.

Variety

Most teachers strive to select a wide range of resources from which their students can benefit. The competitive edge definitely belongs to those who are willing to experiment with an assortment of material and bring variety into their lessons.

Task 1

Look through the selection of resources available for use in your course or program.

1. Where do you look for resources? Rank order the possibilities on the list below.

— They are available on site.
— I adapt and expand on the available resources.
— I borrow resources from a professional resource center.
— I borrow resources from the local public library.
— I buy my own resources.
— I create my own resources.
— I find resources on the Internet.
— I bring authentic materials to the classroom.
— I involve students in preparation of resources.
— Other: _____

2. How often and in what ways do you use the materials and resources listed in the following chart?

	Daily	Occasionally	Never	Only for my own reference	As a source for adaptation
Curriculum guidelines					
Commercial textbooks and workbooks					
Teacher's manuals					
Authentic materials					
Teacher-made materials					
Student-made materials					
Visual aids					
Audio aids					
TV and VCR					
Computer software					
Guest speakers					
Field trips					
Other: _____					

3. Are there some options listed in the preceding questions that you have not used? Why?

_____

_____

4. Are your resources limited? If so, reflect on the reasons, list sources of frustration, and try to think of some solutions.

_____

_____

_____

_____

5. Review the needs assessment you conducted at the beginning of your course. Compare your students' needs and the resources you used over the last week. Do they match?

_____

_____

Characteristics of Resources

The ignorant are always prejudiced and the prejudiced are always ignorant.
CHARLES V. ROMAN, _SCIENCE AND ETHICS_

The past few decades have witnessed a proliferation of commercial teaching and learning resources. While most new publications adhere to current thinking about teaching methodology, not all are appropriate for every group of learners. Further, we must remember that students commonly have a great deal of respect for the printed word, and they trust that everything their teachers bring to the classroom is reliable and correct. It is important that we ensure that our students' trust is not misplaced by reviewing and assessing the materials we use, becoming familiar with their limitations, and ensuring that additional material is available to compensate for weaknesses.

Task 1

This task, adapted from Jadwiga Gurdek's _Materials Evaluation Survey_, may help you evaluate the texts you are currently using.

1. Evaluate the resources you use according to the criteria provided.

	Very much			Very little		
	5	4	3	2	1	N/A
Main text						
The material promotes critical and logical thinking.						
The material reinforces the use of a variety of skills and learning strategies.						

	Very much			Very little		
	5	4	3	2	1	N/A
The text explores all relevant areas of the subject matter.						
The text builds on and expands students' knowledge of the subject matter.						
The text assists students in acquiring knowledge and skills they need for next grade or course.						
The material follows a task-based approach.						
The material has clear and appropriate goals.						
The material and any included tasks prepare learners for real-world activities and challenges.						
Contents are organized into themes and topics.						
A variety of text selections that generate interaction, discussion, or learner response are included.						
Chapters are of an appropriate length.						
The language is clear, authentic (as opposed to simplified or "bookish"), and appropriate for the students' level.						
The material is appropriate for the learners' age.						
Background information is included, where necessary.						
Illustrations and examples are included wherever necessary and are appropriate.						
The material can be easily adapted the suit learners' needs and abilities.						
The material is culturally sensitive and unbiased.						
The material is interesting and enjoyable.						
Workbook						
The content of the workbook has a clear relationship to that of the textbook.						
The exercises adequately reinforce and extend the material presented in the main text.						
The exercises are meaningful and approximate real-life tasks, and provide additional practice for students.						
The workbook contains fun activities (e.g., puzzles, scrambles, games).						
An answer key is included.						

	Very much			Very little		
	5	4	3	2	1	N/A
Teacher's guide						
The teacher's guide clearly identifies the objectives for each unit.						
Essential background information is provided for each activity.						
An abundance of extension or follow-up ideas (e.g., games, quizzes, exercises) is included.						

2. What conclusions can you draw from your evaluation? What are the elements in the resources you use that make them suitable for your current students?

_____

_____

Task 2

Analyze the resources you use in terms of possible bias; their portrayals of different cultural, ethnic, religious, and racial groups; and their depiction of a wide range of people.

The material presents a variety of attitudes and opinions objectively and without prejudice.
Yes ❏   No ❏

The material presents different cultural, ethnic, and religious groups with respect.
Yes ❏   No ❏

Any characters used or people described are not presented as stereotypes.
Yes ❏   No ❏

The illustrations present individuals from a variety of backgrounds and cultures.
Yes ❏   No ❏

No particular lifestyles are promoted over others.
Yes ❏   No ❏

The relationships among people depicted are based on equality and mutual respect.
Yes ❏   No ❏

Women are presented in a variety of roles.
Yes ❏   No ❏

The disabled and the elderly are represented with respect.
Yes ❏   No ❏

Judgmental language (e.g., *primitive*, *lazy*) is avoided.
Yes ❏   No ❏

Task 3

1. How often do you ask your students' opinion of the resources you use?

2. What aspects of the resources do students comment on?

	Usually	Often	Sometimes	Hardly ever	Never
Topic appropriateness					
Level of difficulty					
Appearance					
Format and layout					
Content					
Length					
Other: _____					

3. Together with a colleague, select a textbook or other resource that you both use and discuss it in terms of the points raised in the questionnaire in Task 1 (p. 83). Do your opinions about the resource differ? If so, how?

_____

_____

4. Design a student questionnaire about the resource, using relevant points from the questionnaire in Task 1. What are the results?

_____

_____

Task 4

Photocopiers are available in many schools and program centers and are extremely useful for preparing what are popularly called "handouts." (Note, however, that photocopying of previously published material can be restricted by copyright laws and should be done only with appropriate permission.) However, a teacher once mentioned to us that he preferred to use the word *worksheets*, which he felt invited students to be active in doing the work rather than to receive passively something handed out by the teacher.

What term do you use? How do you feel about it?

_____

_____

Textbooks versus Authentic Materials

Real people don't talk like books.

LUCIA PIETRUSIAK ENGKENT

"Authentic" materials are resources we use everyday that were not prepared originally for purposes of instruction. In the language classroom, such materials might include newspapers, magazines, forms, or brochures written in the target language; in the elementary classroom, a teacher might choose to supplement a commercial reading program with "real" children's books chosen from the library. Such resources can be enormously useful in all types of instruction because they expose learners to real-world materials used in real-world ways.

Task 1

1. Which of these materials do you feel your students benefit most from? Rank them from 1 to 3.

Authentic materials   Commercial materials   Teacher-developed materials

2. Of all the materials you used last week, what percentage fell within each of the three categories?

Authentic materials ___% Commercial materials ___% Teacher-developed materials ___%

3. Compare the ratings from question 1 with the percentages in question 2. Do you provide a good balance of materials?

_____

_____

Task 2

1. Many teachers are stuck with the particular textbooks mandated by school boards, administrators, and other authorities. If this is your situation, how do you use the textbook to best advantage?

— I pick and choose from it.
— I change the sequence of lessons or activities as necessary.
— I adapt lessons and handouts as necessary (remembering to indicate their original source).
— I supplement it with other resources.
— Other: _____

2. Are there other things you could do to improve the way you use the textbook?

_____

_____

Authentic Reading Materials: Newspapers and Magazines

What other teaching resource is more up to date and offers something of interest to more people than newspapers and magazines? In addition, these authentic materials are inexpensive, practical, and, if used effectively, popular with students. At the same time, these materials are easy to misuse.

Picture this scenario:

In an ESL program for adults at a beginning level, the teacher came to class one day each week with a stack of newspapers. The activity was always the same: students were each to browse through a newspaper, read an article, and write a ten-sentence summary. After a few weeks, some of the students could be heard whispering, "Not again!" when the teacher appeared with the weekly stack of papers. The activity seemed to drag on forever, and most of it consisted of a silent vocabulary search that resulted in long lists of words that students obviously could not remember. Across the city, a group of literacy learners was working with the local newspaper. The topic for the lesson was the weather, since a particularly bad storm had swept through the area the day before, and the teacher began by introducing and discussing some weather-related vocabulary. The students' task was to identify weather words in the caption and story accompanying a photograph depicting storm damage. The students opened their newspapers, searched for the article by using the photo as a clue, and highlighted all the storm-related words introduced in the lesson. Their pride at being able to read a newspaper was clearly visible on their faces.

Besides ensuring that the newspaper and magazine tasks we assign are at the appropriate level, we should ensure that we design a variety of activities, so that using this medium does not result in boredom. Newspapers and magazines lend themselves well to activities that focus on skills of skimming, scanning, or detailed reading, and strategies such as guessing, predicting, and making inferences. And, of course, they are also useful sources of information in a broad range of disciplines.

Task 1

1. How often do you make use of newspapers and magazines in your classroom? Circle one.

quite often   occasionally   rarely   never

2. Browse through a newspaper, identify articles you could use with your students, and create activities based on them. Possibilities might include a vocabulary search or puzzle, one group creating true-false statements for another group to answer, individual writing of alternate headlines or photo captions, or group staging of a press conference or debate related to a controversial issue. Keep in mind that students must be armed with strategies for reading any texts that are above their linguistic competence; though they absolutely do not need to understand every word, they should be able to comprehend the gist. (In *Vocabulary*, John Morgan and Mario Rinvolucri suggest a wonderful and very successful strategy for convincing students that they understand more than they think they do. Ask your students to read a text and cross out everything they do not understand, and then to try to make sense of what is left.)

Describe the activity or activities you devise. What makes them particularly useful and meaningful for your students?

_____

_____

_____

_____

Distribution

Decisions about how to distribute materials to students do not have a major impact on the quality of teaching. Nevertheless, as with many "micro" skills, this area deserves some attention since it affects the flow of the lesson.

Task 1

1. Think about your usual manner of distributing handouts or books to your students and the rationale behind it. (If you can, videotape a few lessons and analyze objectively what you do.) Now respond to these statements, indicating what percentage of the time you do the following things.

— I give out materials along with instructions to each student individually. ____%
— I walk around the classroom and give out materials to each student individually. ____%
— I give a stack of materials to a few students at different ends of the room, saying "Take one and pass the rest on." ____%
— I pile materials on my desk and ask students to come up individually to pick them up. ____%
— I ask for volunteers to distribute materials to the rest of the class. ____%
— Other: _____

2. What is your rationale for the option you use most frequently?

_____

_____

3. When do you distribute handouts for a particular activity?

— Before I introduce the activity, because I want students to look at them while I give any explanations.
— As I begin my introduction and explanations, to save time.
— After I introduce the activity, so the students will not be distracted from the explanations.
— Other: _____

4. What is your rationale for selecting the option you use most often?

_____

_____

5. Monitor this area during a few lessons and experiment with different ways of managing distribution of materials. Have you noticed any problems with any of the approaches? Do you find that one is more effective than others?

_____

_____

Technology in the Classroom

Technology has become a part of the classroom furniture. It all started with slide projectors, film strips, overhead projectors, and reel-to-reel movies, and today it has so infiltrated education that it has changed the ways students learn and teachers teach. Gone is the traditional pattern established by textbook, teacher, and chalkboard; welcome to videos and computer-assisted learning.

Task 1

1. What technology do you use regularly in your classroom?

slide projector	teletrainer	VCR
filmstrips	tape-recorder	computer
overhead projector	TV	other: _____

2. Which of the above do you have access to, but have chosen not to use? Why? Did you use those technologies in the past?

_____

_____

Task 2

Despite the fact that the benefits of playing videorecordings in the classroom are abundant and well known, they are actually not that commonly used. The most usual reasons given are that televisions and videorecorders are not readily available, and that teachers simply do not have time to create meaningful video-based activities.

1. Have you attended any workshops on how to use video in the classroom?

_____

_____

90

2. In your preservice program, did you receive any training in the use of video? Was it adequate?

_____

_____

3. Finding out how our colleagues around the globe use resources can be inspiring. The literature is full of useful ideas. For example, in a number of articles Johanna Katchen describes using videos with university-level EFL students in Taiwan. What articles, books, or book chapters related to video have you read?

_____

_____

4. How did you locate them? If you have not read any, where could you find them?

_____

_____

5. If you believe you could benefit from training in the use of video in teaching, do some research into the options. These may include

- a workshop, presentation, or refresher course offered as an inservice professional development program;
- books, articles, or videos from a teacher resource center;
- Internet bulletin boards for teachers;
- colleagues; and
- suggestions from your supervisor.

Which options are possible for you?

_____

_____

Task 3

One inappropriate use of video is to have large groups of students watch long stretches or entire movies together with very little preparation or follow-up. It is impossible to find a full-length video that will engage a large group for its entire duration and is aimed at a level appropriate for all viewers—some learners will invariably tune out. The result is often that students come to see video as a teacher's way of "killing time," and it ceases to be a useful and valid instructional tool.

1. What is your experience with using video in the classroom? Were videos used in any classes you attended as a student?

_____

_____

2. Although full-length movies can certainly be shown effectively with the right group of learners and with appropriate preparation and follow-up, shorter videos may generally be more appropriate. Possibilities include

- short (15 to 20 minutes) commercial videos prepared specifically for educational purposes;
- news clips, interviews, commercials, talk shows, music videos, documentaries, etc., of appropriate length (and recorded after appropriate permission has been obtained);
- short programs (about 20 minutes, without commercials) that can be viewed in segments and thus form a constituent part of several lessons; and
- short programs on topics of interest to students and relevant to their needs.

Have you used any of the above with your students? How successful were such recordings?

_____

_____

3. Video content should be analyzed from the students' perspective. Will your students find it interesting and suitable? How does the content you select relate to students' own circumstances and goals? Do you ask students to discuss the topic prior to viewing, brainstorming ideas and predicting the content?

_____

_____

4. In addition to previewing activities, students need to be provided with a task to complete during viewing. This makes the activity more meaningful because it gives students a clear notion of why they are participating. Can you identify some of the tasks you have used, or list ideas for tasks that could be created?

Video: _____   Task: _____

Video: _____   Task: _____

Video: _____   Task: _____

5. If you have used such tasks, were they effective? How successfully did your students complete them while watching the video?

_____

_____

6. A videotape of your students made during a presentation activity can become a teaching tool in its own right. For example, teachers might record student presentations and ask learners to view the video to analyze their language use and presentation skills. Have you ever created such a learning tool in your classroom?

_____

_____

Computers

Computers in schools and their use in instruction provoke extreme reactions, ranging from enthusiasm to deep resentment. Teachers are generally either enthusiasts ("I can't wait for the new computers!"), mild supporters ("An excellent idea, but we'll need a lot of time to implement it"), quasi-supporters ("An excellent idea, but it won't work in my classroom"), passive resisters ("Not a bad idea, but very impractical"), or fierce opponents ("Another fancy way administrators have found to waste money"). Most of us, however, realize that computers are here to stay, and their role in education will only increase with each new school year. The controversy over their use is beginning to diminish, and remaining opposition will probably turn into quiet acceptance.

This is appropriate, since the benefits of computers as an instructional tool are numerous. Nevertheless, as with any other piece of technology, caution is recommended with computers, too. We must ensure that when we use them we do so meaningfully. Despite all their advantages, the headaches of using this technology are many and varied, for both the teaching staff and the administration. They include the following areas of concern:

- the need for initial teacher training and education;
- the need for ongoing training with new equipment and software;
- substantial initial costs for hardware and software;
- ongoing costs associated with upgrades of hardware and software;
- the need for field-testing and evaluation of hardware, software, and instructional packages;
- problems of reliability; and
- ongoing reliance on technical support.

Some of the advantages and disadvantages related to computer use are explored in the following tasks. Others, related specifically to the context of language teaching, are examined in the next chapter.

93

Task 1

1. Physical arrangements for making computers available to students and teachers vary considerably. Which of the options below best describes the situation in your teaching context?

— A shared computer lab of stand-alone terminals, available on a preset schedule ____
— A shared computer lab of networked terminals, available on a preset schedule ____
— A computer lab of networked or stand-alone terminals, available on a first-come, first-served basis ____
— A single computer in my own classroom ____
— Several computers in my own classroom ____

2. The physical set-up obviously has an effect on how computers can be used for individual, pair, group, or whole-class work, and for in-class, remedial, or homework activities. How do you maximize the opportunities for learning with the options that are available to you?

_____

_____

Task 2

Think about how you present and explain software to your students to ensure that they know how to use the program's features.

1. What teaching techniques and strategies do you use when you present and explain a new software package or any unfamiliar features or functions it might contain? Indicate how often you use each of these possibilities.

— I photocopy and distribute pages from the manual ____% of the time.
— I write up and distribute a simple instruction sheet ____% of the time.
— I provide pairs of students with a strip with instructions ____% of the time.
— Prior to class, I write instructions on the chalkboard or on chart paper placed in a spot visible to everyone in class ____% of the time.
— I demonstrate the software and its functions to the class as a whole ____% of the time.
— I explain to all students while writing step-by-step instructions on the board, and then I circulate to provide support while the students work on their own ____% of the time.
— I demonstrate it sequentially to small groups of students who gather around ____% of the time.
— I provide both written instructions and a demonstration ____% of the time.
— I demonstrate it to every student individually ____% of the time.
— I demonstrate it to a group of high-ability students and ask them to be teacher assistants ____% of the time.
— I work at my networked terminal, and students can see what I'm doing on their own monitors ____% of the time.
— Other: _____

2. What is the rationale behind your usual method of presentation and explanation?

_____

_____

3. If the computers are not in your regular classroom, where and when do you present new software and explain new operations?

	Always	Often	Sometimes	Never
I provide all introductions and explanations before students go to the computer lab.				
I provide a brief introduction in class, but the full explanation is offered while students are seated at computers in the lab.				
I write instructions on the chalkboard or chart paper before students go to the lab, and they copy them down.				
Everything related to computers takes place in the lab.				

Task 3

We often have more students than computers in our classes, and this poses an additional challenge: Who gets to use the computers when, and what do students do when they are not using them?

1. What do you usually do in this situation?

— Two or more students sit together at the same machine.
— One student is seated at each computer, while others work on different tasks; after a predetermined length of time, students switch positions.
— Students are scheduled individually for computer time to perform the necessary tasks.
— Other: _____

2. If you usually follow the second option above, how do you prepare?

— I have the activities ready prior to class.
— I make a decision about activities on the spot, depending on how many students are present in class.
— Other: _____

3. You cannot be in two places at the same time. If some of your students are working on computers while others are in a different part of the room, engaged with other tasks, how do you handle the situation?

— I explain the computer task to the first group who will be working at the computers, then I leave them for a while to explain the other task to the second group (or vice versa); after that I assist whichever group seems to need more help.

— I explain the non–computer-related task, and then leave that group to work on their own because these tasks are usually easier to do than the computer work.

— Other: _____

4. Do you clearly indicate in your lesson plan what each group will be doing and when?

_____

_____

Resources in the Community

You and your students are members of communities that offer a variety of resources. By bringing those resources into the classroom—or bringing your classroom to them—you ensure your students' exposure to the most authentic learning material—people and places from the real world. For second-language learners, speakers from the community afford extra practice in communication and aid in students' processes of settlement and acculturation.

Task 1

Place a checkmark beside the community resources you use in your search for materials for your program.

Community	Resources	How I use these resources
City/town	Municipal offices Cultural and recreational facilities Local newspapers Other	
Neighborhood	Community agencies Community publications Community services Community events Volunteers Guest speakers Other	
The school	Administrative staff Colleagues Other classes and students Other	

Community	Resources	How I use these resources
Other_____	_____	_____
	_____	_____
	_____	_____
	_____	_____

Task 2

Do this task if you include field trips or guest speakers in your program.

1. How do you decide what places to visit or who to invite to your class?

— I choose, according to my preferences.
— I evaluate the "success rate" of previous trips or speakers.
— I pass around a list of suggested sites to visit or speakers to invite, and let students make selections.
— I choose places and people that can enhance the curriculum.
— I plan around students' needs and interests.
— Other: _____

2. How do you prepare for field trips or guest speakers?

— I preteach main concepts and language.
— Students research the place or topic.
— I bring in promotional literature.
— I brainstorm what needs to be pretaught with the guest speaker or staff at the field trip site.
— I make clear to the speaker or site staff the proficiency level of the students.
— I talk to the guest speaker or site staff prior to the event and make suggestions intended to ensure that their presentation is as interactive and appropriate as possible.
— Other: _____

3. If you teach older or more proficient students, do you make them part of the preparation? Do you ever ask them to contact a guest speaker and arrange a session?

_____

_____

4. Complete the following chart.

	Always				Never
	5	4	3	2	1
During the trip or guest speaker's presentation					
Students undertake a task I have planned and explained.					

	Always				Never
	5	4	3	2	1
I make myself available to the students and site staff or guest speaker.					
I monitor interaction and try to ensure that all students participate and are involved.					
I take notes during the presentation so that I can create follow-up activities later.					
Other: _____					
After the trip or presentation					
I ask the speaker or site staff for feedback on how my group reacted.					
I sum up experiences in a follow-up lesson.					
I obtain feedback from students.					
I make notes about any problems or things that should have been done differently, for future reference.					
Other: _____					

5. Is there anything in your use of community resources that needs to be altered? If so, what?

_____

_____

Students as Resources

Students, especially if they are adults, bring to class a variety of experiences that teachers can and should draw on. A nurse from Guatemala in an adult ESL class can teach others about nutrition, healthy living, and her culture; a mechanic from Vietnam has much to share besides expertise in basic car repair. Everybody has something to share—whether it is a talent in music or cooking, a fascinating cultural heritage, or professional knowledge—and we can all learn from that sharing. Further, giving students the opportunity to identify and give what they have to offer puts them in the position of experts and boosts their self-confidence.

Task 1

1. How do you usually identify the expertise and experience your students may have? Can you recall expertise and experience among your students that you have tapped into recently or would like to explore?

Student: _____ Expertise/experience: _____

98

Student: _____ Expertise/experience: _____

Student: _____ Expertise/experience: _____

2. Obviously, students are more motivated to participate in class if they can bring their own background knowledge, experiences, and circumstances into the discussions and activities. This applies to all learners, from beginners to advanced and from preschoolers to adults.

Analyze an activity you are planning to do with your students. What background knowledge might students have that relates to the activity? How can you activate that knowledge?

_____

_____

3. How are you going to make use of this background knowledge? How will using it benefit the students?

_____

_____

Task 2

One way of having students share their expertise and experiences is to arrange for group or individual in-class presentations on appropriate topics and issues.

1. Do you include group, pair, or individual presentations by students in your program? Why or why not?

_____

_____

2. What kind of presentations do you include, and how often?

_____

_____

3. How do you ensure that the audience is respectful and maintains interest?

_____

_____

4. What language and communication skills necessary for presentations do your teach?

_____

_____

5. What tasks do you give your students to complete while listening to the presentations?

_____

_____

6. Do you expect your presenters to prepare handouts or to create tasks for the class to work on before, during, or after the presentation?

_____

_____

7. Do your learners evaluate the presentations?   Yes ❑   No ❑

8. If yes, do you generate the evaluation criteria with them?   Yes ❑   No ❑

9. In what other ways do you invite students to share their expertise and experience with the class?

_____

_____

Task 3

Conduct an experiment in your program. Have your students prepare short group presentations on a topic of interest that they know or want to research. Teach the necessary presentation skills, prepare the venue and the audience, and plan a listening task for class members to complete during each presentation. Observe your students' participation and motivation. Finally, survey your students on their feelings about the process. What are the results of the experiment?

_____

_____

_____

_____

7. Resources in Language Classrooms

The preceding chapter explored resources used by teachers and learners across a range of disciplines and instructional contexts. Language teachers, whether in second- or foreign-language programs, have unique concerns, however, and these are the focus of this chapter.

Commercial Materials

All teachers must assess the quality and content of the commercial teaching materials they use. Language teachers have the added responsibility of assessing their appropriateness in terms of language use and expression for particular students. Many such products attempt to appeal to the widest possible market, sometimes thereby diminishing their effectiveness. Resources for language teachers that present "clinical," bookish formulations of the target language, free of local idioms, phraseology, or semantic features, for example, may well be inappropriate in many language-teaching contexts. And some materials may be geared at an appropriate proficiency level for your students but at an entirely inappropriate age.

Language teachers might want to revisit the tasks under "Characteristics of Resources" in the previous chapter, completing them again with their particular students firmly in mind. In addition, the following task, taken from Jadwiga Gurdek's *Materials Evaluation Survey*, is specifically designed for language teachers who use commercial audiovisual products in their programs.

Task 1

Evaluate the audio- and videotapes you use according to the criteria provided.

	Very much			Very little		
	5	4	3	2	1	N/A
The material follows a task-based approach.						
The selection depicts real-life situations that include different types of speech (formal, informal, colloquial) that can be directly applied in social communication.						

		Very much				Very little	
		5	4	3	2	1	N/A
The language sounds spontaneous and is accompanied by appropriate background noise.							
The tasks approximate the real-world activities of listening and responding to someone or something.							
The pace is appropriate for the learners' level.							

Authentic Materials

The importance of authentic materials as resources for language teaching cannot be understated—indeed, their value has been clearly recognized by almost all experts in the field. Textbooks, workbooks, and other commercially produced teaching aids certainly have a place in second- and foreign-language programs and teachers should by all means use them, but authentic materials bring real-life freshness into the classroom. Through these materials students acquire the knowledge, strategies, structures, and vocabulary they can use in everyday situations. It is considerably more useful to learn how to comprehend a radio weather forecast or traffic report, for example, than to listen to a talk on migrating habits of whales. Some—or even many—students may well find whales interesting, but it is highly unlikely that they are as relevant.

The following story illustrates the benefits of authentic materials in the language-learning environment. Encouraged by an inservice presentation on authentic listening materials, an instructor started taping the morning news each day and developing simple listening tasks and activities for her ESL class of high beginners. A visit to the class on one of the first days of this new approach saw students struggling with the challenging language. But they were persistent in their attempts, particularly when the instructor explained what she was trying to accomplish and asked them to participate in the experiment. Two months later, the results were astonishing. Not only were the students able to cope with the news broadcasts, but most of them had learned correct forms of the passive, and could express their opinions and retell the stories in simple language. They also were more aware of events in their new community, city, and country.

Using authentic materials is not without challenges, of course; we all know how difficult it is to work with resources that are often beyond our students' language proficiency, and it is true that a considerable investment of time and energy is required to assemble and use the materials. However, they are still preferable to a steady diet of simplified, artificial texts and aids that do not reflect the features of "real" language, idioms, and expressions. To use authentic materials well, we must do the following:

- design tasks simple enough for students to undertake successfully;
- explain to students that they need not understand every word in a text in order to get the gist; and
- prepare students by working on necessary skills and strategies.

Task 1

Radio and television broadcasts, along with newspaper and magazine articles, always include opportunities for teaching grammar. Once you make a decision on what type of activity to conduct with such materials, you can analyze the text or a transcript to determine what linguistic structures leap out. By teaching these you ensure that the grammar is embedded in the content, thereby making instruction more meaningful.

1. Select two articles from the same newspaper. Analyze each text and determine what structure could be taught through it. Decide how the structure could be presented and practiced (refer to Chapters 8 and 9, if necessary).

Article: _____

Structure: _____

How it will be presented: _____

Article: _____

Structure: _____

How it will be presented: _____

2. Try out one of the activities and evaluate it with the questionnaire in Task 3 on page 129. Was it successful? How could it be improved?

_____

_____

Task 2

Most radio stations will give you permission to tape and use broadcasts and reports for educational purposes. (The situation with regard to television is more complex. Teachers who wish to videorecord television programming should contact a media specialist in their program, district, or board to determine what restrictions may be in place for such taping.) Tapes can often be used without modification right after recording, but if you have access to two tape-recorders (or one with dual slots), you can create well-organized master tapes of selections from several broadcasts for more sophisticated activities.

1. Have you ever tried to use a news broadcast or any other authentic listening material in your class (weather forecasts, traffic reports, commentaries, advertisements, talk shows, recorded telephone messages, songs, etc.)? If so, how successful was it?

_____

_____

2. Are you able to make authentic listening materials available reasonably easily? If not, does your program have any staff or facilities that might be able to assist you?

_____

_____

3. Have you ever tried to contact a radio station? If not, contact one to see if you need permission to tape programs.

_____

_____

Task 3

How long can you listen to something you do not completely understand? Certainly not very long, and that has to be taken into consideration when you are selecting material for classroom use. Very short news stories are real gems for listening comprehension activities, and a variety of activities can be developed for them (for some first rate ideas on listening strategies, see David Mendelsohn's "There ARE Strategies for Listening").

It is prudent to start with activities that provide a great deal of support. Since the content may be beyond students' level of comprehension, a good strategy is to write key words on the chalkboard. It is essential that they be written in clusters, to provide context—for example, *48-year-old man, armed with a pistol, shot his neighbor in the leg, is under arrest, police officer.* As a prelistening activity, students can work in groups to figure out the meaning of words they do not understand, using all possible strategies. They can then come up with their own version of the story and share it with the class. If the word clusters can be arranged to produce different versions, lively discussion may result. This raises the interest level for listening, as students are keen to find out what really happened. (The word clusters above, for example, could tell a story of a police officer arresting a man for shooting his neighbor—or perhaps it was the police officer who was under arrest....) A variety of follow-up activities are possible: students can write the real story, come up with a list of questions related to other details they want to discover, or use their imaginations to expand on the story.

Try out the described activity sequence. How well did it work for your group of students? What, if anything, needs to be changed to make it more meaningful for them?

_____

_____

Task 4

Since students generally enjoy listening to music, it may be a good idea occasionally to supplement the listening component of your program with popular songs. They can facilitate vocabulary learning and help students pick up idiomatic expressions.

1. How often do you utilize songs?

Several times a week   Once a week   Sometimes   Rarely   Never

2. Who selects them?

My students do   I do   We choose them as a class
The textbooks include suggestions
Other: _____

104

3. If you usually select the songs, what are your selection criteria? Rank the following criteria according to the weight you assign to each.

— performer
— tempo
— topic
— lyrics
— language structures
— cultural appropriateness
— age of learners
— assumptions about learners' preferences
— Other: _____

4. List all the types of activities you use with songs.

_____

_____

_____

_____

5. Which of the activities do you use most often? Why? Is there enough variety in the way you use songs now? Are there some other activities you could try?

_____

_____

_____

_____

Task 5

Students learning a second or foreign language can benefit greatly from videorecordings of authentic materials, usually those broadcast originally on television for native speakers of the target language. For ESL students particularly, getting hooked on an entertaining situation comedy set in their new country or even within the community can provide invaluable insights into authentic language use and the everyday life and culture of native speakers.

If you teach ESL, select a popular sitcom currently on TV in a convenient time slot. Base your selection on the program's target audience, setting, and cultural appropriateness. Once you have obtained any permission required, record several installments and start a cycle of viewing a fragment (no longer than 10 minutes) on a regular basis. Begin with previewing activities (introduction, reading, group discussion, group retelling of the previous episode, etc.) and then play the short segment several times while students complete a simple task. Postviewing activities should cover the spectrum of controlled (vocabulary, grammar) and communicative practice (discussion, role-play, etc.).

Tell your students when they can watch the sitcom on TV at home.

1. Over the stretch of several lessons, note your students' reactions, comprehension, and attitude. What do you observe?

_____

_____

2. Ask your students if any of them have begun watching the program at home. Have you talked to them about it?

_____

_____

Computers in the Classroom

> *We do not feel it is necessary to convince teachers that they should use computers.... Teachers will use them if they are available, if they know how to, and if they see some value in doing so.*
> DAVID HARDISTY AND SCOTT WINDEATT, *CALL*

Computers are a valuable tool for language teaching, but, as is the case with all resources, they must be used effectively. This section, along with the computer-related tasks in Chapter 6, are intended to help you gain insights into using them and to evaluate how well they are being incorporated into instruction.

Throughout this section, we use the acronym CALL, for computer-assisted language learning. This term, used frequently in the literature on computers in language teaching and learning, emphasizes the range of roles that computers can play and does not refer to any single philosophy or approach. In CALL, a variety of software can be employed, and activities can fall anywhere on the accuracy-fluency spectrum, from mechanical through to communicative.

The Historic Perspective

The first model of the use of computers in teaching and learning, developed in the 1960s and 1970s, was referred to as *computer-assisted instruction* (CAI). In terms of the language classroom, CAI could be described as "behavioristic" CALL. Here the computer plays the role of instructor, and the dominant types of activities are grammar or vocabulary drills, practice exercises, and tutorials.

With CAI, the main advantage of the computer over a well-designed textbook is its ability to offer immediate, objective, accurate correction and feedback and to score and keep student records automatically. The model also frees the teacher from the boring, repetitive work of assigning and supervising such activities, and it encourages students to take risks more willingly because they are working alone in a nonthreatening environment, at their own pace, and without peer or teacher interference. However, CAI, with its mechanical drill-and-practice format, was soon criticized for using computers as "expensive page turners."

In the 1970s and 1980s, such criticisms led language teachers and software developers to adopt an approach of computer problem solving with adventure games or simulations. In this model, the computer is a collaborator and stimulates language use. The initiative comes from the students who, for example, must ask the computer questions or select from options in order to win the game or pursue the adventure. The most obvious advantage of this new model is its possibilities for engaging learners in problem-solving activities, alone or in groups or pairs. At the same time, the limited scope of the language practiced within each game or simulation, the lack of software suitable for adult learners, and the high cost of most programs meant that this approach did not become widely popular in language classrooms.

Teachers then began to turn to popular computer applications or programs not specifically developed for the education market. The best examples are the "productivity tools" or office applications such as word-processors, spreadsheets, databases, text analyzers, and communication software. These packages offer the advantage of almost unlimited flexibility, since content is created by the teacher or students. Relevance and student involvement can thereby be ensured. The use of such tools facilitates task-based learning and cooperative group work, and arms students with additional marketable skills in software use. This model remains highly appropriate, particularly for adult ESL or secondary school programs.

Today the focus is increasingly on multimedia and the Internet. They allow the integration of language skills and bring the outside world into the classroom in ways we could never have dreamed of even a few years ago. Once they become widely available, these tools may entirely reshape language teaching and learning.

Task 1

Do this task if you use computers for grammar teaching or as a tool for student practice.

1. Obviously, prior to selecting a student grammar book, we need to make certain decisions about how we will teach grammar in our classrooms. (Chapter 9 in this book discusses these decisions in detail.) Think about the activities included in the computer software you use in the same way you think about activities in a grammar book. How do they compare? What are the advantages and disadvantages of each? What decisions do you have to make prior to conducting the activities?

_____

_____

2. Computers need to be incorporated into language instruction in meaningful segments of carefully thought-out lessons. How do you incorporate grammar software in your program and lessons?

	Always				Never
	5	4	3	2	1
My students work on their own with a tutorial, and cover grammar exercises systematically in the sequence recommended by the tutorial.					
I use the software selectively, according to how particular activities fit into my lessons.					

		Always			Never	
		5	**4**	**3**	**2**	**1**
My students all work on the same part of the program at the same time.						
I assign individual practice depending on students' needs and levels.						
I use the authoring tool in the software to customize the practice and activities it offers.						
Other: _____						

3. Why do you use the method(s) you use?

_____

_____

Task 2

Think about the time your students spend working with grammar software.

1. How much time can your students spend doing exercises and activities in their grammar texts or workbooks without losing interest and attention?

_____

_____

2. How much time can your students spend working on a grammar tutorial or grammar exercises on a computer without losing interest and attention?

_____

_____

3. What conclusions do you draw from the comparison?

_____

_____

Task 3

Do this task in the event you use a software package designed for English-language teaching in your program.

1. Did you select the software yourself, or are you required to use the one selected by supervisory staff or administrators?

_____

2. Who were the primary users the software developers had in mind when they created your package?

EFL preschoolers or elementary level   EFL secondary school students
   students   ESL secondary school students
ESL preschoolers or elementary level   EFL adult students
   students   ESL adult students

Other: _____

3. Like any teaching material, computer software needs to be used selectively and appropriately. For example, ESL students in an elementary school may not find EFL-oriented materials very useful, as they are likely to deal with content of general interest to professionals or advanced students. Similarly, EFL students in Vietnam would probably not benefit from an ESL software exercise about conducting a job search in Toronto. Review the needs analysis you conducted with your students. How do your students' needs and goals relate to the software you use?

How appropriate is...	Very				Not at all
	5	4	3	2	1
the content?					
the range of topics?					
the level?					
the grammar content?					
the English (British, American, Australian or Canadian)?					
the use of language?					

4. What features of this software make it appropriate for your students?

_____

_____

5. Analyze one of your lesson plans and describe what you did to incorporate computer work with this software. Did your students see it as a part of the language lesson, rather than as something distinct? Was it a meaningful activity?

_____

_____

6. In general, how would you rate this software?

Excellent ❑   Good ❑   Fair ❑   Poor ❑

7. How do your students rate it?

Excellent ❑   Good ❑   Fair ❑   Poor ❑

Task 4

1. Have you ever used games or simulations for language teaching? If so, how?

_____

_____

2. How did your students respond? How beneficial did they find it?

_____

_____

3. What criteria need to be employed when selecting games software for the language class-room? How do these criteria compare to those for selecting any other kinds of games?

_____

_____

Task 5

1. Do you use productivity tools or office applications (such as word-processing packages, databases, or spreadsheets) in your program? How?

_____

_____

2. What are the positive aspects of such programs for your particular students?

_____

_____

3. What challenges do you face in making the most of these packages in your classroom?

_____

_____

4. Are the texts, databases, spreadsheets, etc., that your students create related to their personal or school circumstances?

_____

_____

5. If you are not currently using productivity tools or office software in your program, are you familiar with such applications? If not, do you know somebody who can introduce you to them? What kind of training will you need if you decide to pursue using these tools in your classroom? Design an action plan to gain the skills you will require.

_____

_____

_____

_____

Task 6

1. Do you have Internet access at school, home, through the local public library, or somewhere else? Do your students have access?

_____

_____

2. If you or your students do not have Internet access at school or home, can you visit a local library or resource center to be introduced to it?

_____

3. What Internet language teaching resources are you aware of? What Internet sites might your students benefit from visiting? Have you ever used any of them?

_____

_____

4. How could these resources be used in your classroom? Could you create tasks for your students to do while they are on the Internet?

_____

_____

Computers and the Language Curriculum

The purpose of this section on computers is not to be prescriptive; each of the described models of computer use (or a combination approach) may have merits for a particular program or group of students. One of our newer roles in teaching is to determine how computers can help our students' reach their own personal goals. We should not be using computers just because everyone else seems to be doing so, particularly when other media may be as or more appropriate for particular activities. Rather, we should conduct ongoing needs analyses with students and ask them

111

for regular feedback about how the computers and software we use are helping them improve their language skills.

When integrated into a well-organized ESL/EFL curriculum, computer use can have two main benefits: first, the technology is attractive and students usually want to use it, which means that CALL is a strong motivator that can result in improved learning; and second, computer skills acquired through language learning can be used outside the classroom setting. The effectiveness of computer use in the language program depends on how computer and language tasks are combined. If the computer work is meaningful, aimed at accomplishing a relevant goal, some language use will follow naturally. For example, any of these activities could be conducted equally well in an ESL, EFL, or first-language classroom:

- Students use word-processing software to access scrambled stories the teacher has prepared, related to the topic currently being discussed in class. They use cut and paste tools to find the correct sequence. As a follow-up, they create their own scrambled stories and make them available on disks for their classmates.
- Students create a flyer advertising an upcoming school or class event.
- Students interview each other and create a class profile using a spreadsheet or database.
- Students create graphics and text for a class presentation, using a word-processor or presentation software.
- Students gather name and address information from students in the class, enter it into a data file, and merge it with a letter they write to invite everyone to a class party or celebration.

In the particular context of the language-teaching environment, however, there are other aspects of CALL we should keep in mind. Effective instruction will be characterized by

- the use of a variety of interaction patterns;
- information- and opinion-gap tasks;
- practice along the entire fluency and accuracy continuum;
- a stress-free atmosphere; and
- a clear link between the language and computer components of the program.

Task 1

1. If you teach both ESL/EFL and computer skills in your program, describe one of the activities you use that combines the two. Evaluate the activity in terms of how meaningful the language and computer components are.

_____

_____

2. If you have more students than computers, what type of language activities do those waiting for their turn at the computers do?

Language activities	Always	Often	Sometimes	Never
Grammar				
Listening activities				

Language activities	Always	Often	Sometimes	Never
Speaking activities related to the topic dealt with in the language class				
Silent reading				
Writing				
Group work related to the topic dealt with in the language class				
Other: _____				

3. What is the rationale for the option you usually select?

_____

_____

Computers across Proficiency Levels

The use of computers can enhance learning for students at all levels of language proficiency. At lower levels of proficiency, computers allow students to work individually, progressing in private at their own level and pace in a nonthreatening environment. At higher levels, more challenging activities that necessitate solid computer skills and considerable creativity are needed to keep students motivated. Whatever the level, the opportunity to learn computer skills is valuable in increasing students' knowledge about new technologies and fills them with increased self-esteem.

It often happens that students' level of language proficiency does not match their computer skills. Beginner-level ESL/EFL students may be quite familiar with a variety of software applications, while more advanced students may struggle even to turn on their computers. But just as we work to help students improve their language proficiency no matter the level, so too can we focus on developing computer skills with all our learners.

Task 1

1. Think about the composition of your current class. Determine both your students' language proficiency and their level of computer skill.

Student name	Language proficiency	Computer skills level

Student name	Language proficiency	Computer skills level
_____	_____	_____
_____	_____	_____
_____	_____	_____
_____	_____	_____
_____	_____	_____

2. Most teachers end up with a class of mixed proficiency and ability levels. If this is your situation, what impact does it have on your lesson planning? How does it affect group work on the computer-based tasks?

_____

_____

3. Teaching a mixed-proficiency ESL/EFL class with some focus on computer skills poses an extra challenge and often causes frustration. One way of keeping everyone happy is to use the same method you generally do in any language class: have an extra language activity or computer challenge handy for those students whose proficiency enables them to complete assignments ahead of the others. Another idea is to ask students with strong computer abilities to become teacher assistants. This gives them additional opportunities to use the target language and boosts their self-esteem.

Look at your last lesson plan. How do you address everyone's needs? Can you identify any extra activities that you prepared? If you didn't have any such activities available, what could you have designed?

_____

_____

The Effectiveness of Computers for Language Learning

It is probably fair to say that CALL is still searching for its place in the language classroom. In general, any technology well used in a language program can serve to bring students together to interact, negotiate meaning, solve problems, and work out strategies for accomplishing the task at hand. In some programs where CALL is emphasized, an additional goal is to combine development of language and computer skills. In that case, a computer class never ceases to be a language class, and vice versa.

Task 1

There is a definite shortage of quantitative studies on the effectiveness of computer technology for language teaching and learning. Teachers who use computers, however, testify to positive student reactions to CALL and increases in student motivation and enrollment. Positive comments outweigh negative ones even when students must work on repetitive and seemingly boring grammar tutorials.

What are your observations about your students' attitudes toward computers?

_____

_____

Task 2

In *Computers in Applied Linguistics: An International Perspective*, Martha Pennington and Vance Stevens report that studies analyzing second-language talk at the computer indicate clearly that students converse a great deal more in regular conversational or speaking activities than they do when working on computer tasks, even in pairs or small groups.

Some ways to foster such communication include

- encouraging students to help each other (in the target language, of course);
- encouraging higher level students to assist lower level ones;
- designing tasks so that students have to share information in order to tackle and complete them; and
- providing each student with only half of an instruction sheet, thereby forcing pairs to work cooperatively and assist one another.

Observe your students doing a computer task. (If possible, audio- or videotape the interaction of one group or pair.) Analyze the students' interaction according to

- patterns of interaction;
- length of interaction;
- turn-taking during interaction;
- language structures used; and
- other aspects that become evident.

1. What do you observe?

_____

_____

2. Which strategies did you use to promote student interaction? Are there other strategies that you think might be effective?

_____

_____

8. Elements of a Lesson

What is the difference between a good meal and a solid lesson? None, since both must include fresh, well-balanced ingredients, selected according to the consumers' preferences and needs. Successful lessons incorporate numerous ingredients essential to the learning process. Balance of those ingredients determines the quality of the lesson—which, in turn, determines the level of learning and the resulting student satisfaction. We must therefore make time for frequent contemplation of how the elements of our work in the classroom fit together. Decisions regarding preparation, delivery of instructions, classroom language, presentation techniques, and pacing are numerous, and each requires reflection. It is essential that we consider how all the possible options may affect our lessons—and students—before we actually step into the classroom.

There are no magic formulas for conducting effective lessons all the time. The reflection process might therefore appear quite elusive, particularly to novice teachers. Still, it is a highly beneficial undertaking, as it makes us better able to predict what might happen in the classroom and thereby to anticipate some potential problem areas.

This chapter is intended to encourage you not only to give attention to the quality of each of your lesson elements and the way they all work together, but also to evaluate your performance after lessons are completed and to establish goals for improvement. The next chapter discusses some elements of lessons unique to the language-teaching environment.

Presentation Techniques and Language

Two presentation techniques, inductive and deductive, were illustrated in Chapter 5 on lesson planning (see pp. 63). Additional aspects of presentation may include your choice of language and manner of speaking, the use of teaching aids, and your physical position in the classroom. (The latter is explored in greater detail in Chapter 3, where it is presented in the context of use of classroom space.)

Task 1

1. Identify what you do in the classroom to ensure that students can hear and understand you and that their attention is held during your presentation.

	A lot		Not at all		
	5	4	3	2	1
I vary my presentation techniques to include both inductive and deductive approaches.					
I use both aural and visual aids.					
I present concepts in a natural context.					
I monitor my voice to ensure clarity, audibility, and appropriate speed.					
I change position in the room—sometimes standing at the front, sometimes at the side, and sometimes circulating.					
I check with my students to make sure that they can all hear me well.					
I vary the tone and melody of my voice.					
I check frequently to ensure that my students understand the concepts I am presenting.					
I use an appropriate level of language.					
Other: _____					

2. Which points above are your particular strengths? How are you going to address the weaknesses?

_____

_____

_____

_____

Task 2

Experts agree that, regardless of the level of learners, a teacher's language must be comprehensible and authentic, rather than artificial and unlike what one would hear outside the classroom. It has to be clearly articulated but should also expose students to new vocabulary, structures, expressions, and idioms. This is true for all classrooms but may be particularly important in foreign- or second-language programs, where students need to get used to the manner and speed of utterance of native speakers of the target language.

1. How do the points above relate to your use of language in the classroom?

_____

_____

2. What do you think teachers should keep in mind about the use of language in the classroom?

_____

_____

3. Monitor your language during presentations for the next few lessons. (If possible, do this by video- or audiotaping yourself and preparing transcripts of a few segments during which you spoke at reasonable length.) Are you actually doing what you thought you were doing? What are your strengths and weaknesses in language use?

_____

_____

_____

_____

Giving Instructions

In order for an activity to be effective, students must understand the instructions. We have all had the experience of preparing solid activities that turn out to be less than successful because students did not understand what we wanted them to do. When we know that an activity is strong, we are often tempted to rush ahead to start it without adequate explanation, or we fail to plan how instructions will be delivered.

Giving solid instructions for a task does not involve special know-how, but it does require planning in advance of each activity. Self-evaluation guided by the checklist in Task 1 and the videotaping in Task 4 may be particularly effective in helping you to assess and improve your skills in this area.

Task 1

To ensure that all students understand the instructions, are on task, and are able to keep up with the class, which of these actions do you usually perform?

	5	4	3	2	1
I plan my strategies for explaining the task before I come to class.					
I wait to get attention from all my students before I start to deliver instructions.					
My instructions include information to ensure that students are absolutely clear about what they are supposed to do and why and are provided to all students simultaneously. I avoid repeating them to individuals while distributing handouts or books.					
My instructions are concise, clear, and ordered in a logical sequence and I support verbal instructions with visual aids and demonstration, if necessary.					
I am cautious about when I distribute books or other materials or ask students to open their texts, because I do not want to distract them from listening to me.					
I tell students how much time will be allotted to the activity.					
I make statements to trigger students' background knowledge related to the activity.					
I do a trial run through the activity with a group of students to provide an example.					
I don't assume that students have understood the instructions, but rather check directly that they have done so by asking *them* to explain what they are supposed to do.					

Task 2

Investing time in planning how instructions will be issued pays off in the long run. By constructing a clear picture of what needs to be explained and how, teachers avoid the scenario in which students spend the first five or ten minutes of the activity floundering in confusion and asking their classmates or the teacher for help. After all, when this does happen, the teacher has to come up with clearer instructions anyway. For students, unclear instructions mean time must be spent searching for strategies to decode the task, and obviously the opportunities for learning presented within the task itself may be obstructed.

1. Select an upcoming activity and plan the instructions. What are you going to do and say? Go over the list in Task 1 and note the actions you plan to perform.

_____

_____

2. Did rereading the list prompt you to think about any areas where there is room for improvement in your own practice?

_____

_____

Task 3

Students, like teachers, "acquire classroom experience"—for them, this means learning how to learn and becoming familiar with different types of activities. "Experienced" learners usually need less explanation and less time to carry out variations on familiar tasks. New activities, however, should be allotted more explanation and time since students are learning both *from* the task and the task *itself*.

Do you consider this when introducing activities? Think of the last time you used a type of activity you and your students had never used before. Did any problems occur? If so, was there anything you could have done to avoid them?

_____

_____

Task 4

1. Video- or audiotape one or two of your activities. While viewing or listening to the tape, focus on how you gave the instructions. Examine the list in Task 1 one more time, and note the actions you actually performed before your students plunged into the activity. (If taping is not possible, try to self-evaluate right after you conduct an activity.)

_____

_____

2. Check the tape again and focus on your students. Are they doing what they were expected to do?

_____

_____

3. Was anyone asking questions or looking for clarification? If so, what insight does that give you? Could anything have been done differently?

_____

_____

4. What impact would a different approach have had?

_____

_____

5. How would you rate your instructions about this activity for this particular group?

   5   4   3   2   1
Very effective   Not effective

Types of Activities

One good way of tackling the problem of boredom in the classroom is to use a wide variety of activities. This variety must be logical, however; a lesson needs to include a sequence of activities and techniques with a common objective.

Task 1

Review your lesson plans for the past two weeks and note the types of activities you used. Possibilities might include

brainstorming	pair work	finding similarities/differences
role-play	problem solving	guessing game
hands-on manipulation	questionnaire	opinion poll
discussion	dialogue	drill
lab activities and demonstrations	storytelling	matching
artwork	questions and answers	cloze or fill in the blanks
songs	sequencing	vocabulary practice
puzzles	guided writing	free writing
scanning	skimming	comprehension check
reading aloud		completing a worksheet

1. Was there enough variety in the activities you conducted?   Yes ❑   No ❑

2. Circle any activities on the list above that you are not familiar with. Where could you find out about them?

_____

_____

3. Are there activities on the list that you rarely or never use? If so, which ones? Why?

_____

_____

4. Is there any type of activity that you really feel uncomfortable doing? Why?

_____

_____

Task 2

Think about the activities you used in the past two weeks and consider the following questions.

1. Did they focus on both form (controlled practice such as grammar exercises, arithmetic drill, questions and answers, true and false statements, matching, etc.) and meaning (discussion, unrehearsed role-plays, interviews, surveys, group problem solving, etc.)?
Yes ❑   No ❑

2. What was the balance of teacher-directed versus student-centered work?

Teacher-directed ____%   Student-centered ____%

3. Was this balance reasonable and effective?
Yes ❑   No ❑

4. Were the students involved in problem solving?
Yes ❑   No ❑

5. Did you facilitate all students' participation during the activity and in the report-back phase?
Yes ❑   No ❑

Preparing Students for Activities

It is the supreme act of the teacher to awaken joy in creative expression and knowledge.
ALBERT EINSTEIN

Not only do teachers need to prepare for activities—so do students. An activity cannot be effective if students are not provided with all the tools necessary to perform it. As David Mendelsohn points out in an article in *TESL Canada Journal*, "If we simply create situations and opportunities for practice in our classes without teaching the students to do that which we are teaching, then what we are doing is not teaching at all, but rather testing."

Task 1

One way of finding out whether you have done sufficient preparatory work with your students is to evaluate an activity right after it is completed, and then brainstorm how you could profit from any errors in preparing your students when you next conduct a similar activity.

1. How much time did you spend preparing your students for the activity?

5 to 10 minutes   10 to 20 minutes   20 to 30 minutes   More than 30 minutes

2. What information, areas of the subject matter, skills, and strategies related to the activity did you preteach?

_____

_____

3. Was the preparation time enough?
Yes ❑   No ❑   Almost ❑

4. Were most students able to cope with the activity without difficulty?
Yes ❑   No ❑   Almost ❑

5. Did you monitor the process?
Yes ❑   No ❑

6. Were students able to transfer and use knowledge gained before the activity in completing it?
Yes ❑   No ❑

7. If your response to any of these questions was no, why?

_____

_____

8. In the activity, were you teaching or testing?

_____

_____

9. What, if anything, would you do differently next time?

_____

_____

_____

_____

Task 2

If learners are not prepared for the activity, the result is stress and frustration. Students respond to activities better if they know what they can expect and feel comfortable with the skills and material that have been pretaught.

1. How do you help your students lower their level of stress and frustration?

_____

_____

2. Have you ever noticed your students hesitating about starting work on an activity? Perhaps on occasion they leaf through their notebooks or books, look around in confusion, ask their classmates for help, or complain to each other. How would you describe the atmosphere? How do you think they felt?

_____

_____

3. How did you react? Was your reaction appropriate?

_____

_____

4. Do you remember experiencing stress in your own days as a student because you felt underprepared to accomplish an activity? What could your teachers have done to minimize this stress?

_____

_____

Pace

Classroom activities are not unlike visits from dear out-of-town relatives. When they drag on too long, what began as the best of times can turn into a nightmare. And when they are too short, you feel that many stories you wanted to share remain untold.

To understand aspects of how to pace our teaching, we must consider the classroom experience. Novice teachers tend to cut an activity off when the time they had planned for it has elapsed; as a consequence, they can pass up opportunities to capitalize on students' interests. With experience, teachers learn to gauge their activities, continually checking how students are responding and developing a sense of exactly when to stop one activity and move along to the next. However, as David Mendelsohn wisely points out in "Making the Speaking Class a Real Learning Experience," we all "have a tendency to let an activity go on for too long, particularly when it's a good one or one we've put a lot of work into." He suggests that we learn to stop "while students still feel 'I would have liked a little more of this.'"

Task 1

1. For your next lesson plan, use the chart below to note the time you plan to spend on each activity. As the lesson unfolds, mark the actual time spent. After the lesson, reflect on any digressions

125

and the rationale for them, and re-evaluate the time originally allotted to each activity. (If possible, videotape your lesson, and then view the tape to determine the time spent on the activities, the digressions, and possible ways to revise your pacing.) Note comments about pacing the activities on your lesson plan for future reference.

Activity	Time allotted	Time spent	Digressions	Why?	Revised time allotment
_____	_____	_____	_____	_____	_____
_____	_____	_____	_____	_____	_____
_____	_____	_____	_____	_____	_____
_____	_____	_____	_____	_____	_____

2. Your students will certainly be willing to provide you with feedback on pacing. After one of your next lessons, explain to them that you want to ensure appropriate pacing, and ask them to complete a survey indicating whether each activity in the lesson was much too long, a little long, just right, a little short, or much too short. Analyze the survey results to determine whether the majority of the students feels there was a pacing problem in the lesson.

Task 2

A French teacher gave the adult students in her multilevel class a crossword puzzle to complete as a warm-up activity at the beginning of a lesson. The majority completed the task within the planned twenty minutes and started talking among themselves—which would have been good practice in conversation, except that they were speaking in English. Meanwhile, a few students were still trying to complete the puzzle. The activity dragged on for almost an hour, with the teacher going from one lower level student to the next to offer help. Her feeling was that these students, whose self-esteem was already low, would have felt badly had they not been able to finish the puzzle.

1. What would you have done in this situation?

— I would have done what this teacher did.
— After the allotted time, I would have had students check their answers with other students, so that all would have obtained correct responses.
— I would have paired lower with higher level students.
— I would have given out two crossword puzzles of different levels of difficulty.
— I would have prepared an extra activity for higher level students.
— Other: _____

2. What would the rationale for your action(s) be ?

_____

_____

126

Task 3

Even experienced teachers can misjudge the time required for a certain task. It often happens that some students finish well ahead of others, but we should never allow an activity to drag on because we can think of nothing else to do with the class. Experienced teachers usually plan additional tasks in case some or all students are able to complete an activity more quickly than planned, or they create two related activities, one easier and a second more challenging. They also develop a repertoire of review activities that need no introduction and may be used in conjunction with particular lessons—"just in case."

Analyze again (on videotape, if possible) one of the activities analyzed in Task 1.

1. How many students finished the activity before the allotted time?

2. Did they actually complete it, or did they simply lose interest?

_____

3. What were they doing after they finished?

_____

_____

4. Did you notice any signs of boredom?
Yes ❑   No ❑   I don't know ❑

5. What did you come up with to keep the learners who finished early busy and interested?

_____

_____

6. If you have a multilevel class, what impact does that have on pacing?

_____

_____

Task 4

1. Think back to your days as a student. When you did not participate in a lesson, what were the reasons?

— The lesson was too easy.
— I found the lesson too difficult or overwhelming.
— The lesson was not interesting.
— The lesson was not relevant to my needs.
— I simply did not want to participate.
— I did not like the teacher.
— Other: _____

127

2. What did you do?

_____

_____

3. How will you address the same problem in your class?

_____

_____

Activity Evaluation

Unfortunately, there is no "undo button" on the classroom keyboard—all we can do is try "restart" the next time around. The effects of an activity that did not bring the desired results cannot be reversed, but we can ensure that the same thing does not happen again. Since we all seem to learn best from our own mistakes, one way to do this is to analyze an activity that did not work well with your students. Tasks 1 and 2 following are related in general to such an activity; subsequent tasks will help you consider each of the activity's stages.

Task 1

Reflect on why an unsuccessful activity was not productive and consider how it could be altered. (If you cannot remember any such activity, keep this task in mind to use when you realize that something has "bombed.") Alternately, if you have already video- or audiotaped lessons for completion of earlier tasks, select the tape that contains the least successful activity and evaluate it by answering the questions below.

1. What was the activity's objective?

_____

_____

2. Did the whole lesson ultimately direct students toward this objective?

_____

_____

3. Describe what you were doing during the activity.

_____

_____

128

4. How would you define your role? Do you think anything related to your role needed to be altered?

_____

_____

Task 2

Imagine that you have found an excellent newspaper article that contains a great deal of information relevant to the unit you are teaching. Unfortunately, the text is above your students' comprehension level and contains considerable unfamiliar vocabulary. If you decide to use the article, you will need to make some decisions *prior* to conducting the activity:

- What will be done as an introduction?
- How are you going to deal with the reading aspect? Will you read the text aloud? Will students read silently? Will students take turns reading one or two sentences aloud? Will that be done with the whole class or in groups? Will students be allowed to read silently prior to reading aloud?
- How are you going to deal with vocabulary? Will you ignore teaching it directly and instead concentrate on strategies of guessing and predicting? How will you explain to your students that they do not need to understand every word to get the gist of the text?
- In the event you want to present the vocabulary, how will that be done? Will students have access to dictionaries? If not, will you answer individual vocabulary questions while students read? Or will you perhaps ask students to make a list of unfamiliar words to be discussed after everyone has read the text?
- When discussing the vocabulary, will you present all of it on the chalkboard? Or will you present only selected vocabulary? Or will students work on it in pairs or groups?
- Finally, what is the task that students will do in relation to this text?

When planning an activity, most teachers think in terms of the first and last questions, and tend to neglect the ones in between.

1. Reflect on decisions you made while planning the unsuccessful activity analyzed in the preceding task. How detailed were your decisions at the lesson-planning stage?

_____

_____

2. What can be the consequence of not making decisions prior to class?

_____

_____

3. Select a text to work on with your class. Now, neglect all the planning stages except the last one, and identify only the task itself. Conduct the activity, and observe your process of decision making as you move along (or later, on a videotape). What decisions are you forced to make? What impact do they have on the class? What impact would different decisions have had on your class?

_____

_____

Task 3

Now do a detailed, stage-by-stage evaluation of the activity. Again, if you have the activity on tape, your analysis can be considerably more objective.

1. What introductory activity did you do to focus the students' attention?

_____

_____

2. What strategies were your students expected to use to complete the activity? How did the warm-up prepare students to use the strategies successfully?

_____

_____

3. In setting the task, were instructions concise, clear, and specific enough? How do you know?

_____

_____

4. Were all your students absolutely clear about what they were supposed to do? How did you check this before starting the activity?

_____

_____

5. Was the activity engaging for your students? Did all of them participate?

_____

_____

6. If interaction was part of the task, did this go well?

_____

_____

7. In your follow-up, did you elicit students' reactions to the activity? Did you check if they enjoyed it? What part of it did they find most useful?

_____

_____

8. Was the activity set at the right level—challenging enough, but not too difficult for the majority of students? If not, how could it be modified to better suit your students?

_____

_____

9. Was it well paced? What do you think is the most effective length of time for this activity?

_____

_____

Task 4

Now consider where your students' problems with the activity originated, with a view to improving your facilitation.

1. Which cues helped your students perform the activity?

_____

_____

2. Where did the students have trouble?

_____

_____

3. What help did they ask for?

_____

_____

4. If the activity involved a text, how did you deal with new concepts, vocabulary, or comprehension problems?

_____

_____

5. What follow-up activities did you do?

_____

_____

Task 5

Finally, think of ways the activity could have been improved.

1. Based on your responses in the preceding tasks, can you identify the reason(s) the activity was unsuccessful?

_____

_____

2. If so, how could you revise the activity, knowing what you do now?

_____

_____

3. What areas do your students need more practice with before you undertake such an activity again?

_____

_____

4. Did your students suggest variations to the activity? Did you ask them to?

_____

_____

9. Elements of a Language Lesson

Besides the considerations raised in the tasks presented in Chapter 8, teachers in each subject discipline have their own specific concerns. Discussed here are issues related to teaching second or foreign languages: preparing students for language activities, constructing activities to ensure balance among the skills addressed, and register. The chapter concludes with an in-depth examination of teaching grammar in the language classroom.

Preparing Students for Communication

When we make ourselves understood, we always speak well.
MOLIÈRE, *LES FEMMES SAVANTES*

Communicative activities cannot be carried out effectively unless preparatory work has paved the way and provided students with required skills. Without those skills, students may be able to communicate only with truncated, broken language. For example, if a teacher wants students to learn how to leave a telephone message, he or she needs to preteach quite a few language items. If students are not comfortable with the following aspects of language use, it is likely that they will not be able to complete the activity successfully:

- expressions—ways of introducing oneself on the phone ("This is.... calling"; "speaking," etc.)
- functions—polite requests ("Could you please tell her that....")
- grammar—reported orders ("Please ask her to...."); for higher level students, structure such as embedded questions ("Could you let me know when you are planning to....")
- vocabulary (*touch-tone phone, leave a message after the beep*, etc.)

Mistakes made during preparation always come back to haunt us during an activity. And it is not just a question of ensuring that students have the necessary skills: we must also ensure that they understand the language we use to describe how the activity will be performed.

133

TEACHER-CENTERED CLASSROOM VS STUDENT-CENTERED CLASSROOM

Task 1

Select a communicative activity and evaluate it right after you have done it in class. You might like to do this in conjunction with Task 1 in the student preparation section of Chapter 8 (see p. 123).

1. What grammar points, vocabulary, functions, or expressions needed to be pretaught? Were they adequately addressed in your preparatory work?

_____

_____

2. What other aspects of language needed to be pretaught? Were these adequately covered?

_____

_____

3. Were most students able to produce appropriate language to complete the activity without difficulty?

Yes ❏   No ❏   Almost ❏

4. Were students able to use the language items you pretaught?

Yes ❏   No ❏

5. If your response to any of these questions was no, why was this the case? What might you do differently next time?

_____

_____

Task 2

It takes expertise and practice to stage an effective activity. Tips from specialists can help you design activities to provide the most benefit to your students. For example, in his *Teaching by Principles*, Douglas Brown emphasizes that, among other things, activities need to be "short and sweet." Do you agree? Why? Why not?

_____

_____

Balance of Skills

Second- or foreign-language acquisition depends on acquisition of four skills: reading, writing, speaking, and listening. Students at different stages of their learning path or in different learning contexts may need more emphasis on particular skills. For example, new immigrants to English-speaking countries need basic oral survival skills first, while university students studying German as a foreign language may need to learn how to tackle sophisticated texts. Establishing the skills that need to be addressed should be an aim of the initial needs assessment for each program and group of learners. Unless your program is dedicated to a specific language skill (French conversation, for example), you should examine your learners' different needs and then balance the skill areas addressed in your activities.

Task 1

1. Reflect on the balance of skills in your last few lessons. Use the circle below to create a pie chart, with each "slice" indicating the percentage of time you allocated to each of the four language areas.

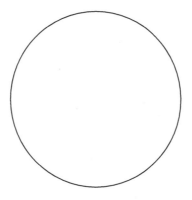

2. How does the time allotment indicated in your pie chart correspond to the needs analysis you conducted at the outset of your program and the program's overall goals? Are your students getting what they need?

_____

_____

_____

_____

Register

Some teachers believe that the purity of the target language should be protected in the classroom, while others feel that today's colloquialisms are tomorrow's standards. In "Real People Don't Talk Like Books," Lucia Pietrusiak Engkent claims that register is often neglected in language teaching. Indeed, many ESL materials smooth over register differences to offer students a "homogenized" model of English.

Task 1

Look at the materials you used in several of your recent lessons and respond to the following questions.

1. What register do your materials model?

informal (colloquial)   consultative   formal

2. What register do you emphasize when teaching spoken language?

informal (colloquial)   consultative   formal   depends on context

3. What sorts of differences in register do you point out to your students?

— grammar (e.g., "There's lots of people here" vs. "There are many people here")
— pronunciation (e.g., "wanna be" vs. "want to be")
— ellipses (shortcuts) (e.g., "the Net" vs. "the Internet")
— spelling (e.g., "tonite" vs. "tonight")
— euphemisms (e.g., "little girls' room" vs. "washroom")
— slang (e.g., "pretty bad" vs. "quite bad")

4. List some examples from your lessons in which you pointed out differences in register.

_____

_____

5. How do you teach when certain registers are appropriate?

_____

_____

6. When do you teach social and cultural conventions associated with conversation in the target language (e.g., handshaking, eye contact, conversational distance or "personal space," etc.)?

_____

_____

7. If you teach ESL or EFL, do you tell your students that tenses in both spoken and written English (especially in Canada and the United States) are not always used the way they are presented in grammar books (for example, the simple past is often substituted for the present perfect)? What implications does this have for your lessons?

_____

_____

8. Pietrusiak Engkent explains that "People appear to be sensitive to errors in register, maybe even more so than to errors in grammar." For example, if an ESL student asks his school principal, "Are you want to speak to me?" it is more acceptable than if he says, "What's up?" What is your experience? How do you bring this issue to your students' attention?

_____

_____

Task 2

Most idioms are directly related to register. Students (especially at higher levels) are usually eager to learn as many idioms as possible, even if they do not quite understand how to use them. The rule of thumb we need to teach is that if students are not absolutely certain of the appropriate context in which to use idiomatic expressions, they should instead use plain language.

1. Do you point out the possible embarrassment speakers might feel if they use an idiom incorrectly? How do your students react?

_____

_____

2. Unfortunately, many textbooks that include sections on idioms present each expression followed only by its meaning and a one-sentence example. The idiom is completely isolated from context, and unless the teacher explains other ways of using it, provides additional examples, and creates opportunities for students to practice in meaningful communicative activities, there

137

is danger of considerable misunderstanding and confusion. What is your experience with teaching idioms?

_____

_____

_____

_____

The Grammar Dilemma

Though this be madness, yet there is method.
WILLIAM SHAKESPEARE, *HAMLET*

The Latin proverb *Tempora mutantur et nos mutamus in illis* ("Times change and we change with them") could best be interpreted for language teachers as "Times change and so do approaches to grammar." The past fifty years have witnessed major shifts in approaches to teaching the structure of language. With these shifts came frequent misunderstandings, including one that suggested "absolutely no grammar, please." Those of us in the language-teaching trenches were confused, often left in the dark or at the mercy of interpreters of the methodologies, who sometimes seemed unable to tell us where grammar teaching was really headed.

Although some confusion remains even today, in general teachers seem much more confident about how to deal with structures than they were twenty years ago. One could say that the position on teaching grammar has softened. Both top-down and bottom-up processing are now acceptable, and these approaches should be used to supplement each other.

We seem increasingly to be embracing an approach in which teachers themselves decide how to teach grammar and how to determine the right proportion of structural and language components, based on needs analyses and taking into consideration a number of classroom factors. Adult language students, for example, are usually quite structure oriented, especially if they have had past language-learning experiences in which grammar was heavily (or even exclusively) emphasized. Teachers may find it difficult to persuade these students that communication revolves around meaning, not structures. On the other hand, younger students may resist any teaching of grammar, finding it confusing, difficult, and dull.

Task 1

In "Grammar Pedagogy in Second and Foreign Language Teaching," a "classic" in the literature on teaching grammar, Marianne Celce-Murcia offers guidelines (see Figure 2) on how to make informed decisions about grammar based on a number of variables. She also explains that though we need to bear in mind that the importance of grammar varies from group to group, it is never unimportant.

Figure 2

	LESS IMPORTANT ←	focus on form →	MORE IMPORTANT
Learner variables			
Age	Children	Adolescents	Adults
Proficiency level	Beginning	Intermediate	Advanced
Educational background	Pre literate, no formal education	Semiliterate, some formal training	Literate, well educated
Instructional variables			
Skill	Listening, reading	Speaking	Writing
Register	Informal	Consultative	Formal
Need/Use	Survival communication	Vocational	Professional

1. Analyze Figure 2 and circle all the key words that refer to your current group of students. Then think about how much grammar you need to teach.

2. What are your conclusions?

Age group of my students	
Their proficiency level	
Their occupations (if adults)	
Their language needs related to communication	
Their language needs related to grammar	
Other:	

3. How do you explain to your students that the main reason for learning grammar is not to be able to recite the rules but to communicate meaning?

_____

_____

The Place of Grammar across the Curriculum

Many types of curricula are in use in language programs: structural, notional, functional, communicative, task based, or various combinations of these. Regardless of the curriculum, however, grammar has a place in it.

Task 1

1. Determine the place of grammar in the curriculum you are currently following.

Is the grammar component explicit?
Yes ❑   No ❑   To some extent ❑

Does the curriculum suggest a particular sequencing of grammar items?
Yes ❑   No ❑   To some extent ❑

Does the curriculum suggest spiraling of grammar items?
Yes ❑   No ❑   To some extent ❑

Does the curriculum suggest techniques and ways of teaching grammar?
Yes ❑   No ❑   To some extent ❑

Are you allowed to make your own decisions about teaching grammar, based on the needs analysis you conducted?
Yes ❑   No ❑   To some extent ❑

2. Do you suggest any changes to the curriculum with respect to its inclusion of grammar?

_____

_____

Task 2

Now consider your long-range plan or course outline.

1. Did you ascertain what grammar points your students lacked prior to creating a long-range plan?   Yes ❑   No ❑

2. If you answered "yes," how did you do it?

— I gave my students grammar books and asked them which units they were not familiar with; then I created a list of priority items and based my plan on it.
— I gave the students a formal grammar test to see what they knew.
— I assessed their knowledge informally by observing their classroom interaction.

3. Which of the following statements are true for you?

— I teach grammar systematically according to a plan, and I build my program around it.

— I check the structures that appear in the topic currently being taught, explain them as they come up, and practice them.
— I monitor the sequencing of grammatical structures in my course.
— I spiral grammatical structures in my program, going back to review ones previously taught.
— I follow the needs analysis to make decisions about teaching grammar.
— Other: _____

4. What is your rationale for these decisions?

_____

_____

5. How do you determine that you are following the right course of action?

_____

_____

Teaching Grammar

Teachers must decide not only how much grammar a certain group of students needs, but also how it will be presented. The tasks that follow deal with this latter issue, a consideration that has become one of the most controversial issues of language teaching for novice and experienced teachers alike—namely, what technique to use when explaining grammar.

Task 1

1. Which of the different techniques below do you use or consider effective for teaching grammar? Enter a check mark in either of the final two columns to indicate your response.

	Techniques I use	Techniques I consider effective
Grammar rules are the starting point, no matter what content is taught.		
Rules are explained orally and the structure practiced, first in a controlled and then in a less-controlled fashion.		
The structure is presented on the chalkboard, followed by controlled and then less-controlled practice.		
The structure is presented orally or on the board, grammar exercises are provided, and then other activities—not necessarily related to the grammar component—are done.		

	Techniques I use	Techniques I consider effective
The structure is presented through content but is not formally taught; after that, students practice it through communicative activities.		
The structure is presented and explained through content, and then students practice it through communicative activities.		
Students are provided with several examples from the content currently being taught and are guided in discovering the grammar rules; after that, they undertake grammar exercises and communicative practice as a follow-up.		
When the structure comes up, it is explained, and students are supplied with rules; they then analyze how the structure is used in context and, as a follow-up, they use it in communicative activities		
Other: _____ _____		

2. Is the technique you use most often the same as the one you consider the best teaching method?

_____

_____

3. Analyze your last lesson and determine which of the options you used. Was it effective and meaningful?

_____

_____

4. What do you do when presenting grammatical explanations?

— I keep explanations brief and clear.
— I avoid using terminology that may be confusing to lower level students.
— I teach and use grammar terminology with higher level students.
— I use visual support to illustrate what I am trying to explain (time lines, stick figures, etc.).
— I list exceptions if necessary. (If so, how many?)
— I illustrate points with numerous clear examples.

5. To identify your approach to teaching grammar, complete the chart below.

		Very important				Not important
When teaching grammar, how important do you think it is to:		5	4	3	2	1
keep it embedded in a meaningful context?						
include it as a cornerstone for communication in your class?						
refer students to solid grammar books?						
teach rules?						
try to maintain a good balance of grammar instruction and communication?						

6. Based on your responses to the preceding questions, analyze the way you present structures and reflect on whether you feel that anything in your approach needs to be altered.

_____

_____

_____

_____

Task 2

Elizabeth is teaching an advanced ESL class of relative newcomers to an English-speaking country. The class is held in a community center, and is part of a noncredit ESL program operated by the local board of education. Her students are mostly young or middle-aged adults with the equivalent of secondary or postsecondary educations. Their goals center around obtaining the level of English required for them to enter their professions and trades in their new country, or for enrollment in retraining programs that would lead to their being able to do so.

Elizabeth appreciates the fact that once a week several copies of a local daily newspaper are delivered to her classroom. She uses them in a variety of ways. The objective of today's lesson is to enable students to comprehend newspaper headlines and to obtain information on current events; the passive voice and the reduction of sentences into phrases as in newspaper headlines are the grammar components Elizabeth plans to review and expand on. After the usual greetings, small talk, and review, the lesson proceeds as follows.

**Introductory activity: Headline scavenger hunt.** Elizabeth selected the headlines that contained reduced sentences in the passive voice and prepared a question about each one. For example, for the headline "Father of Two Killed in Accident," the question was "Who was killed?" The questions were arranged in a different order than the sequence of the headlines in the paper. Students, working in pairs, scan the paper quickly to answer the questions by finding the appropriate headline and noting the page. In a class discussion, Elizabeth quickly takes up the answers to the questions with the whole group.

Precommunicative activity: Individual reading. Students silently read the first paragraphs of the articles attached to the headlines from the scavenger hunt. Elizabeth takes up the reading with the class. Concepts and vocabulary are explained and discussed.

Precommunicative activity: Headline expansion. Two student pairs work together to make full sentences from the abridged headlines, using the knowledge gained from the reading task. For example, "Father of Two Killed in Accident" becomes "Ron Meaker, a father of two small children, was killed in an accident on highway 401 yesterday."

Explanation: Class brainstorming. Students discuss the sentences together. Elizabeth guides them in formulating the rules for creating passive sentences and for reducing full sentences into headline phrases. The "discovered" rules are written on the board. Students take notes. Elizabeth also discusses situations in which the passive rather than the active voice might be used. During an individual grammar practice that follows, Elizabeth sums up the rules for passive voice transformations for all the tenses. Students work on a grammar exercise Elizabeth prepared for the lesson, in which they must transform active voice sentences into the passive.

Communicative activity. Students work in groups to scan several newspapers, looking for more passive-voice headlines. They select one example and present a one-sentence summary of it to class. The other students then role-play reporters asking for more details. Elizabeth encourages students to use the passive voice as much as possible.

Follow-up. In preparation for the next day's follow-up, Elizabeth cuts out several introductory paragraphs from news items. Students work in groups to write headlines for the paragraphs, using abridged passive-voice sentences. When the headlines are taken up with the whole class, students try to come up with fuller versions. This gives students one more chance to review the rules and use of the passive.

1. How do you assess the approach taken here in view of the questions and points raised earlier in this section? How would you define this teacher's approach to teaching grammar? What feedback would you give her regarding the effectiveness of her approach?

_____

_____

2. If you were teaching the same group, would you teach the passive voice in the same or a similar way? Why, or why not?

_____

_____

Task 3

Certain units and topics simply lend themselves to teaching certain structures. If you do not follow a predefined curriculum, one way of deciding on the sequence of units and topics is to use a chart such as the one below as a starting point. Keeping in mind that easier grammar points need to be taught first, units that naturally include those less-challenging structures would then be taught at the beginning of a course. The resulting course outline would be meaningful and would also integrate grammar components logically.

Consider the example below and brainstorm what other units or topics could be linked with what structures. Then use the chart as a basis for sequencing units and topics in your long-range plan.

Unit/Topic	Grammar concepts
Orientation: everyday routines	Present simple, past tense
Housing: neighborhood, apartments and houses	Prepositional phrases describing location, modals (can, allowed to)
Employment: job interviews	Modals (should or shouldn't), past modals for higher levels (should have done/shouldn't have done)
Media: newspaper stories	Passive voice
Past events: childhood	Past tenses, irregular verbs, "used to," "would" for past habitual actions
Other: _____	Other: _____

Using "Traditional" Grammar Exercises Effectively

Most teachers try to teach grammar communicatively—that is, as text rather than sentence based, and embedded in the context or topic they are currently dealing with—but they find that during the controlled stage of the lesson, students need controlled practice. Numerous books on the market provide students with exercises for such practice. They are not, however, "ready to go," and teachers must do more than simply make a decision about which exercises on which page will be used. During the planning stage, time should be spent brainstorming how the activity will be done, regardless of how controlled it may be. Needless to say, if teachers want to avoid unanticipated questions, they must be quite comfortable with the content and answer key.

Task 1

Reflect on what you do before, during, or after the practice stage, and on how you get yourself and your students prepared for grammar exercises.
— I decide which exercises are going to be used ahead of time.
— I decide ahead of time whether students will do the exercise in groups, pairs, or individually.
— I do the planned exercises myself first to determine what problems may arise.
— I check whether anything needs to be explained before students start doing the exercise.
— I prepare the answer key.
— I take up the answers with the whole class.
— I encourage students to make a link between the structure I am teaching and a parallel structure in their own languages.

145

Task 2

There are numerous ways of increasing student interaction even when they are doing traditional sentence-based exercises drawn from grammar books.

1. Try cutting up the answer key and providing each student with a card containing only one or two of the answers. To obtain the other answers, students have to interact with their classmates. Within seconds you have communication in class, and you become a facilitator instead of merely the provider of correct answers.

Experiment with this method and reflect on how it works in your class.

_____

_____

2. Another effective technique for exercises with verb infinitives in parentheses is to use the same text to create two handouts—one has verbs missing from the first part, while the other has verbs missing from the second. Students are given the handouts and must obtain verbs they are missing from their partners, then together decide what tenses to use. This creates an information-gap situation, and students find they must work together to complete the activity.

Have you ever tried to create such grammar exercises? How did they work?

_____

_____

3. Exercises such as those described in questions 1 and 2

- illustrate how "traditional" grammar activities can be adapted to foster communication;
- encourage teachers to think in terms of how interaction can be fostered, even in case of structural exercises; and
- highlight that grammar exercises are not isolated items but rather fit logically into the topic of the day and into the components of the lesson plan.

As with any other classroom activity, a warm-up activity and a review are needed prior to doing even text-based exercises. As a follow-up, students can write paragraphs on a topic similar to that presented in the text-based exercise. Therefore, while doing lesson planning, we must ask ourselves the following questions:

- How can grammar best be incorporated in the content I am now teaching?
- What structure is already embedded in the text or activity of the day?
- What could be done as a warm-up and a follow-up to the grammar exercise?

Analyze a grammar activity you have done recently in light of these points. How effective was it?

_____

_____

Task 3

Opportunities for improvement and growth are maximized by using video or audio evaluation. Try to tape yourself during a grammar activity or exercise. Review the tape several times, and respond to the questions below in light of your analysis and the points raised in this section of the chapter. (If taping is not possible, try to answer these questions right after you conduct a grammar lesson.)

1. How would you evaluate yourself?

_____

_____

2. Is there anything in your approach to teaching grammar that you would like to change?

_____

_____

3. Create a questionnaire to obtain feedback from your students on the way you teach grammar. You might inquire about such things as

- how much grammar you teach,
- when you teach grammar,
- how you present and explain grammar, and
- what grammar practice your students prefer.

Grammar and You

It is not uncommon for native speakers to be unable to articulate clearly the principles of grammar of their language. Regardless of whether you are a native or non-native speaker of the language you teach, it is important to have a clear understanding of the grammar of that language.

Task 1

Assess how knowledgeable you are in grammar.

1. Are you able to answer all your students' questions about various aspects of grammar?

Yes   To some extent   No, but I can find the answers   No

2. Do you consider grammar one of your stronger or weaker points? Is there room for improvement?

_____

_____

3. If grammar is not a strength, what areas could you work on?

_____

_____

4. How do you make yourself better acquainted with grammar?

— I have taken a course in language structure.
— I have carefully looked through numerous grammar texts to familiarize myself with the aspects of grammar explained and to improve my knowledge.
— I have a good grammar reference and always look up the answers to questions I cannot answer.
— I ask colleagues for answers to puzzling questions.
— Other: _____

5. Of the items in question 4 that you did not check, how many would you actually like to do? Create an action plan about how you will do it.

_____

_____

_____

_____

Task 2

1. What do you do if your students come up with a grammar question you do not know how to explain?

	Always				Never
	5	4	3	2	1
I ignore the question, pretending I didn't hear it or changing the topic.					
I give any answer regardless of whether I know it is correct, because I do not want to lose face.					
I ask if anyone in class can provide the answer.					
I tell students that I will address the question as soon as I find the answer.					
I refer students to a grammar text.					
I guide students in finding the answer in a reference text.					
Other: _____					

2. What is your rationale for selecting the option you select most often?

_____

_____

Task 3

1. Learning from our peers can be a powerful tool for improving teaching skills. Consult with a colleague, discuss grammar teaching issues, and fill out the chart below.

Structure	How did you teach it?	How does your colleague teach it?
_____	_____	_____
_____	_____	_____
_____	_____	_____
_____	_____	_____

2. Compare your views and approaches with those of your colleague. What are the similarities and differences in the way they teach grammar? What techniques of theirs would you like to try out? What insights did you gain by sharing your experiences?

_____

_____

_____

_____

10. Classroom Communication

One of our jobs as teachers is to help students identify and achieve their own educational goals, and an element necessary for future success is the ability to communicate and cooperate well with others. Meaningful interaction should therefore be one of the cornerstones on which classroom work is built.

At various times during a lesson, students may be involved in individual, pair, or group work, or they may do whole-class activities or listen while the teacher or another student makes a presentation. Each of these patterns of interaction is valuable, and students benefit from variety and balance among them. This chapter discusses how to assess whether that balance is being achieved and whether the interactive situations in your classroom are successful. Also included is a section for language teachers that explores the difference between "interactive" and "communicative" activities and discusses specific concerns for their teaching context.

Patterns of Interaction

Task 1

Reflect on the interaction patterns you facilitated in your last few lessons. Use the circle below to create a pie chart indicating the percentage of time, on average, your students spent in individual, pair, group, and whole-class activities.

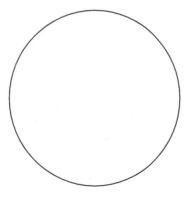

Now sum up your observations.

1. Do you vary patterns of interaction?

Yes ❏   No ❏   Not always ❏

2. How do you encourage pair, group, and whole-class interaction?

_____

_____

3. How do you encourage team work?

_____

_____

4. In "The Dynamics of the Language Lesson," N.S. Prabhu claims that a classroom is an "arena for human interaction." How does this apply to your class?

_____

_____

_____

_____

Task 2

Teachers are human, and some (ourselves included) may tend to talk too much. After all, we always have something *very* important to say! A possible rule of thumb for establishing a balance of teacher and student talk is "If a student can say what you want to say, try not to say it yourself, but make sure you repeat or clarify what the student says so that everyone in class understands."

1. Could this rule be applied in your class? To what extent?

_____

_____

2. Try to determine if, in general, you are a "talker."

— People say I talk a lot, but I disagree.
— People say I talk a lot, and I agree.
— No one has ever commented on the amount of talking I do, so I assume my talk time is well balanced.
— People say I'm too close-mouthed.

3. How much do you think you talk in class?

More than necessary ❑   Only as much as necessary ❑   Less than necessary ❑

4. Is there a clash between your answers to questions 2 and 3? If so, why?

_____

_____

5. Record a representative segment from a lesson. Play back the recording and use a stopwatch to time the teacher and student talk. Do the data prove or disprove your responses to the preceding questions?

_____

_____

6. If you feel you are perhaps too talkative in class, try to minimize your talk time for several days. What impact does this have on class interaction?

_____

_____

7. Survey your students. How do they feel about teacher and learner talk? Do they feel there is a balance in your class? Do they think that student talk is valuable and conducive to learning?

_____

_____

Group Work

It is only in the past thirty or forty years that educators have discovered and come to appreciate the potential of group work. Regardless of the benefits, however, there are still many traditional "teacher-fronted" classrooms, and many students (especially adults and children from various cultural backgrounds) may be unfamiliar with how to work in a group.

To introduce your students to group work, you might begin by explaining some of its benefits. In *Getting Students to Talk*, Aleksandra Golebiowska lists several:

- It generates more student talking time than any other technique.
- It frees the teacher to teach more effectively.
- It is learner-centered and thus actively involves all learners.
- It makes learners responsible for their own learning.
- It is beneficial to the development of group dynamics (p. 6 in *Getting Students to Talk*).

To these could be added

- It allows for more natural student-student interaction rather than just teacher-student interaction.
- It frees the students from dependence on the teacher.

Task 1

1. How do you form groups? Rank order the options below according to how often you use them.

— Students choose whom they would like to work with.
— Groups are determined by the seating arrangement and never changed.
— I group students according to a single criterion (e.g., age, ability level, etc.).
— I group students according to different criteria at different times.
— We do a group-forming activity or game.
— Other: _____

2. What criteria do you apply for group formation? From the list below, choose the five options you use most frequently, and write the percentage of time you use each of them.

— random grouping ____%
— need for groups of a certain size ____%
— seating arrangements ____%
— ability ____%
— students' own selections ____%
— friendship ____%
— common interests ____%
— age ____%
— level of education (for adults) ____%
— ethnic origin ____%
— native language ____%
— deliberately mixed ____%
— Other: _____ %

3. What single criterion do you use most frequently to group your students? Why?

_____

_____

4. Experiment in a few upcoming lessons by using grouping criteria that you do not usually use. Do they work well? Is there a need for change in the criteria you use?

_____

_____

154

Task 2

Random grouping incorporates a positive element of surprise: students never know who they will be working with, and are usually quite accepting of their groups. The drawback, however, is that the teacher can only guess how the particular groupings will work.

1. Indicate which of the following procedures for establishing random groups you have used.

— Students "number off" or are each given a color, letter, etc., and form groups according to numbers, colors, or letters they share.
— Students are asked to get together with others wearing something of the same color.

— Groups are determined by alphabetical order of first or last names: the first four students form one group, the second four the second group, etc.
— Students are asked to find others with whom they have never or rarely worked, who live close to them, who like the same type of food, etc.
— Each student is given a piece of a picture (related to the topic being taught) and has to get together with students who have the other pieces.
— Other: _____

2. Is there a technique that you have not used but would like to try?

_____

Task 3

This task is related to group size.

1. What is your preferred number of students in a group?

    3   4   5   6   more than 6

2. Why?

_____

_____

3. Try to change that number during your next teaching day. Monitor what difference this makes. How did it affect the group work in regard to student talk and task completion?

_____

_____

Task 4

Grouping by ability has different benefits and drawbacks. Equal-ability groups ensure that weaker learners are not inhibited by more able ones, who themselves are not held back by

155

weaker peers. Mixed-ability groups allow students to learn from one another and give students at higher proficiency levels a chance to enjoy being "experts."

If you use ability grouping, what are its strengths and weaknesses for your learners? If you do not, might your students benefit from it?

_____

_____

Task 5

1. Use the chart below to evaluate group dynamics and the quality of participation of individual students in one of your next lessons. Observe group interaction carefully or, if possible, video- or audiotape the group activity. We suggest that you focus on just *one* group so that you can monitor interaction during the whole activity. After the lesson, ask the students in that particular group to complete the chart as well. If you taped the activity, play it back. If you had to complete the chart again, would you circle the same numbers?

	Yes				No
	5	4	3	2	1
All group members contributed equally.					
Students were truly involved and motivated.					
Students found the activity interesting.					
The atmosphere within the group was positive and conducive to learning.					
Students were communicating well and clearly.					
Students were using newly acquired information or skills.					

2. Use the points in the chart to develop a survey for your students to solicit their opinions and attitudes about group work. What are their responses?

Task 6

Reflect on the things you do in order to make efficient use of the time devoted to group work.

1. Do you define the activity for the whole class and avoid explaining it to each group individually?

Yes ❑   No ❑   Not always ❑

2. Do you circulate while your students are performing the activity?

Yes ❑   No ❑   Not always ❑

3. Circle the word that best describes your role when you circulate.

consultant   helper   observer   controller
other:

4. Check with your students. Do they see you in the same role as you see yourself? Would they like you to assume a different role?

5. Do you initiate the group interaction, or do the students?

_____

_____

6. In what cases do you involve yourself in the group's interaction?

_____

_____

7. Do you take note of errors students make while working on the activity?

Yes ❑   No ❑   Not always ❑

8. If you do, do you follow up with activities to assist students in correcting those mistakes?

Yes ❑   No ❑   Not always ❑

Dealing with Learner Differences

Most of us daydream on occasion of an ideal class of uniform students with no individual differences. The fact that, in reality, every group consists of learners of different abilities, preferences, needs, and backgrounds puts considerable demands on us. At the same time, though, it does make our job interesting and challenging. After all, if our students were all the same, we could be replaced by computers, couldn't we?

Ensuring effective interaction in a group of multilevel students is a juggling act—we cannot make everyone happy at the same time, and someone will always have to compromise. There are, however, ways of attempting the impossible.

Task 1

In an excellent book on teaching multilevel classes, Jill Bell (1988) suggests that we select a common topic for all groups but set the activities at different levels. This helps students develop a feeling of belonging to the class and fosters group identity. Collaboration within and among groups is another frequent result, and this gives students the opportunity to get to know all their classmates so that they feel comfortable working in different groupings over the course of the program or semester.

What is your experience of multilevel classes? What strategies have you found to be successful?

_____

_____

Task 2

There are various ways to ensure that most (if not all) students in your class are busy and challenged and that everyone receives individual attention.

1. Look at the list below and indicate the techniques or approaches you have found most beneficial in ensuring that all students receive some individual attention. Think about which ones you have used recently.

	Very beneficial				Not beneficial
Technique	**5**	**4**	**3**	**2**	**1**
Assigning frequent partner or group work					
Circulating during partner or group work					
Encouraging helpful, knowledgeable students to work with less proficient ones on occasion					
Journal writing					
Providing individualized tasks					
Designing activities at different levels of complexity that allow students to work at their own level and pace					
Providing follow-up activities for higher level students (lower ability students may do them as homework)					
Having a stock of extra activities on hand					
Using learning centers so that students can choose activities					
Other: _____					

2. Do you think that each of your students feels he or she is getting enough individual attention to ensure that his or her needs are met?

Yes ❑   No ❑

158

3. If you answered "No," what will you do to better accommodate these students?

_____

_____

Team Building, Racial Tensions, and Conflict Resolution

*If what is preached in the world's churches, synagogues, mosques
and temples was practiced by even a quarter of folks who heard it all
said—what a different planet we would have.*
JOHNNETTA B. COLE, *DREAM THE BOLDEST DREAMS*

Classrooms today are increasingly diverse places. Among our goals, therefore, should be promoting sensitivity to and understanding of different cultures and values.

Task 1

Understanding of different backgrounds and support for a diversity of students begins with raising awareness of distinctive features of cultures represented in your classroom. Some features relate to deeply ingrained value and belief systems, while others are manifested in behavior, clothing, and habits.

1. What differences can you identify among your students pertaining to the following?

Eye contact: _____

Conversational distance: _____

Body language: _____

Use of time/punctuality: _____

Physical contact: _____

Attire: _____

Loudness of speaking: _____

Other: _____

2. Imagine that you are one of your students who is a member of a visible minority. List several barriers or difficulties that this student may experience in your or any other class because of his or her background.

_____

_____

3. What have you done or could you do to assist this student?

_____

_____

Task 2

Experienced teachers are often able to maximize opportunities for developing positive attitudes toward other cultures, thereby minimizing the possibility of classroom conflict arising from intolerance or ignorance of cultural differences. Think about what you do in your classroom to build rapport among students, eliminate racial tensions and discrimination, and encourage mutual respect.

1. Have you been able to create a harmonious classroom environment?

_____

_____

2. What could you do to reduce negative attitudes and interactions?

_____

_____

3. Do you use activities that encourage students to interact and mingle with peers of backgrounds different from their own?

_____

_____

4. Through the material you use, do you sometimes offer your students a vision of the world from a perspective different from their own?

_____

_____

5. How do you encourage students to further one another's cultural education in the classroom?

_____

_____

Task 3

Consider how you may have handled conflict in the past.

1. Have there been any incidents of conflict, racial tension, or discrimination in your classroom recently? If so, how many? What type of incidents?

_____

_____

2. Consider one incident in particular. How did you react?

_____

_____

3. In how many cases were you satisfied with how you handled the incidents? In how many cases were the involved students satisfied with the results or solution? What conclusions can you draw that might help you deal with such situations in future?

_____

_____

_____

_____

4. To familiarize yourself with different cultures and prepare yourself to handle possible negative incidents, which of the following have you done?

— Attended workshops
— Taken a course
— Read appropriate literature
— Consulted with colleagues
— Sought advice from consultants or specialists in the field, social workers, etc.
— Approached appropriate groups in the community
— Other:

Dealing with Discipline Problems

Four high school teachers are sitting in the staffroom. One murmurs, "Oh, gosh!" The second looks at her knowingly and sighs. The third nods his head, adding, "Terrible, huh?" The fourth stands up abruptly and says, "That's it! I can no longer listen to your discussion about discipline problems!"

Students and teachers alike live in today's hectic world of rapid change, of too much work, far-flung and broken families, alienation from community, and widespread violence. No wonder discipline is becoming a burning issue and one of the main causes of frustration for teachers, especially those working in elementary and high school environments in large cities.

If you teach in such a setting or are faced with issues related to discipline in your classes, you know that there is no magical way to deal with the inevitable problems. Instead, you must possess a repertoire of tools and techniques for different occasions.

Task 1

1. The advice in the following list comes from both experienced teachers and high school students. Think about your own strengths and weaknesses in relation to disciplining, and place an *S* or *W* beside each item to indicate how well it relates to you.

— Be consistent in everything you do.
— Do what you preach.
— Don't just set the rules—stand by them.
— Apply the same rules to everyone in class—no favoritism.
— Decide what you want to accomplish, reveal these goals to the students, and act with conviction.
— Make your expectations clear to everyone (and, again, be consistent).
— Plan enough activities to keep students busy, and have extras ready for those who finish early.
— Try to make activities interesting and relevant to students' needs.
— Try to demonstrate understanding for your students, but at the same time be firm (especially at the beginning of a course).
— No matter what, do not loose your calm.
— Use a firm voice, but do not yell or scream.
— Do not confront an unruly student in front of the class, but rather talk to him or her in private.
— Use humor to dissipate tension and frustration.
— Involve the student, parents, and school administrators in conflict resolution, if you can.
— If you're having a bad day, do not bring it to the classroom.
— Don't take things personally.

2. If you noted any weaknesses, which would you like to correct first? Create an action plan to work on this area.

_____

_____

_____

_____

Task 2

Videotape a few random lessons. When you play back the tape, focus on student behavior and your reactions. Were there instances of misbehavior? If so, analyze the segments and answer the following questions.

1. What happened? What did the student(s) do? What did you do?

_____

_____

2. Can you determine the reason for the misbehavior?

_____

_____

3. How could this behavior be prevented in future?

_____

_____

4. Are you pleased with your handling of the situation?   Yes ❑   No ❑   To some extent ❑

5. If the situation were repeated, would your reaction be different?

_____

_____

Task 3

The chart below contains a list of some cues related to student behavior. Have you observed these (or others) in your classroom? How do you interpret them? Complete columns 2 and 3 to help you consider possible ways to react to such behavior in future.

Student cues	Your interpretation	Possible reactions
Students talk while I'm talking.		
Students look confused.		
Students are disruptive.		
Students ask others for help.		
Students write while I'm talking.		
Students flip through their notes.		
Students nod their heads.		
Students look around.		
Students laugh while I'm talking.		
Students yawn.		
Students leave their desks.		
Students don't do what is expected of them.		
Students are lethargic.		

Task 4

For many of us, student misbehavior is our main frustration. For some, it affects and upsets us so deeply that we find ourselves on a one-way street: we can neither determine the causes, nor find effective solutions. That is when peer consultation and observation can help, or at least relieve some of the tension.

If you are in such a situation, enlist a colleague in an experiment: each of you videotape one or two of your lessons, and then exchange tapes. While watching them, you can both refer to the questions in Task 2. As a follow-up, offer each other a constructive analysis and advice pertaining to reactions and strategies that could be used more, and those that could be used less.

Classroom Confidence and Trust

> *Trust thyself. Every heart vibrates to that iron string.*
> RALPH WALDO EMERSON, *ESSAYS*

Classroom confidence and trust is the invisible web that bonds students with one another and the teacher, that supports everyone with the knowledge that teaching will match learning, that emotional support is always available, and that things can and will get done effectively. Classroom confidence is a response to students' concerns of "Can we do it? Can we get results? Is help going to be there when we need it?" and teachers' questions that ask, "Can we manage this? Do the students (and their parents) respect and support us? Are they committed enough?" We know confidence and trust are there when our students say, "We really missed you!" after a substitute teacher has taught for a day. When they are lacking, the result is dissatisfaction on the part of both teacher and students and a frustrating feeling that the program or course is not enjoyable or beneficial enough.

Even though many teachers manage to build classroom confidence and trust with every group of students, they cannot achieve it to the same extent each time. Seasoned practitioners can all recall groups of students that just "clicked" with them right at the beginning of a course, and with whom bonds were strengthened in each new lesson. They also most probably remember at least one group for which it took a painstaking length of time to establish a solid relationship.

An experienced observer can sense the level of classroom confidence within ten minutes of entering a teaching setting; it can be felt in the air and seen on the teacher's and students' faces. Needless to say, students have a sixth sense for it, too.

Task 1

Classroom confidence involves several ingredients that help intensify class ties:

- building your own confidence—looking and acting confident, being aware of who you are and what you can do (the confidence you project is contagious);
- building your students' confidence—awareness of who your students are and their abilities, providing opportunities for students to feel confident about their work, reinforcing the reason you are all in the classroom; and
- building confidence that class work can and will get done—possession of the necessary knowledge of the subject matter and teaching methodologies, determination to achieve your goals.

1. Try to rate yourself on each of the "building" elements listed above.

Building my own confidence

    5   4   3   2   1
Excellent   Poor

Building students' confidence

    5   4   3   2   1
Excellent   Poor

Building confidence about class work

    5   4   3   2   1
Excellent   Poor

2. Which of the three building skills is your strongest? _____

3. To what extent do you feel that classroom confidence is present in your class?

_____

_____

4. If you feel that the level of confidence and trust could be improved, think about the three building elements and come up with an action plan for accomplishing this.

_____

_____

_____

_____

Special Considerations for the Language Classroom: Facilitating Communication and Bilingual Classes

Interaction is important in all educational settings, but in the language classroom it has particular significance in that it is only through interaction that students can learn to communicate in the target language. For language teachers there are a number of options available for enhancing classroom communication. Imagine, for example, that you want to foster interaction through an activity involving a text related to the topic you are currently teaching. You might decide to do any of the following:

- design a group or pair activity in which every student has the complete information;
- cut the text into pieces equal to the number of students in each group and ask students to share information in order to complete the task;
- organize an "ask around" activity in which each student is provided with one piece of information and all must share in order to carry out the task (e.g., fill in the blanks, short-answer questions);
- provide each partner in a pair with a version of the text in which different language items have been deleted, and ask pairs to reconstruct the text by asking each other questions; or
- organize a jigsaw activity in which four groups of equal size each read a different segment of text, and then new groups are formed that consist of students who have read different pieces of information that must be shared in order to do a task.

You may have noticed that all but the first activity have a common feature: they include the information-gap element, and because of it, they can generate genuine interaction among students and could be labeled "communicative activities." Students may certainly interact if you follow the first option, but since they already have all the information they need, they may communicate only because the teacher tells them to do so. It is well accepted that in order to create opportunities for communication that resembles "real life," the information gap needs to be included in language activities.

Task 1

1. During the past week, how many activities involving the information gap were included in your lessons? Was there a good balance?

_____

_____

166

2. How effective do you find information-gap activities in your class? How do your students respond to them?

_____

_____

Task 2

In "Communicative Language Teaching," David Nunan discusses the results of a study indicating that even when teachers are knowledgeable about the principles of communicative activities, "traditional patterns of classroom interaction rather than genuine communication" (p. 137) often continue to dominate. That is, the teacher initiates communication, the learner responds, and the teacher follows up.

Videotape an activity that you had labeled communicative. Watch the recording and try to analyze the patterns of interaction by noting everyone who speaks and timing the length of their communications.

1. What patterns of communication do you see on the tape? Did anyone dominate the conversation? Who initiated the conversation? How would you define your role? Is there a good balance of student and teacher talk? How similar is the pattern of conversation to communication in real life?

_____

_____

_____

_____

2. How content are you with the student interaction in your class? Do you need to change anything in your patterns of interaction to maximize communication among students?

_____

_____

Task 3

Several years ago, I [Hanna] was teaching a class of adult students preparing for TOEFL (Test of English as a Foreign Language). A certain score is required for admission to most postsecondary institutions and, for students seeking to have prior training recognized, to obtain accreditation by professional associations. The majority of my students were at quite a low level of general language proficiency, particularly considering their educational and career goals. In class, however, they did not want to tackle any tasks that were not straight out of the TOEFL book or sample tests. To introduce an element of real life into the program as a way of developing general language proficiency, I resorted to "marketing" strategies, convincing students that although they were listening to the news or reading and discussing an item from a magazine, they were still practicing things that were tested on TOEFL. I found myself saying things such as, "The magazine article you will now read contains interesting uses of the passive voice " and "The conversation you will now hear illustrates the emphatic use of the present subjunctive."

Do you ever have to market your activities? How do you do it?

_____

_____

Task 4

A teacher of adult ESL classes commented that it can be quite challenging to facilitate interaction or discussion when all the students happen to come from the same place (Hong Kong, in the case of her program). For teachers in this situation it is advisable to select communicative activities carefully, keeping in mind that only if students do not have the same information or share the same knowledge or opinions will their interaction resemble real-world communication. Again, the importance of the information-gap component cannot be over-emphasized.

If you teach a relatively homogenous group of students, try to remember a speaking activity that worked well. What were the features of the activity that made communication possible?

_____

_____

Task 5

Bilingual classes are foreign- or second-language classes in which the teacher and students share a language other than the target language, and some instruction is delivered in that language. This situation is common in foreign-language instruction; for example, a teacher of high school Spanish in the United States may conduct at least some portion of the course in English, which is probably the native language of most of the students—and perhaps of the teacher, as well.

In the context of second-language teaching, bilingual classes may be formed intentionally or inadvertently (when, for example, a program in a particular location draws from a homogenous population of new immigrants). There are some obvious advantages when the teacher speaks the first language of the students: learners' feelings of apprehension are reduced, and breakdowns in communication can be quickly remedied. However, in such classes students and teacher may rely too much on the shared language. Sometimes even the most experienced teachers fall into the trap of paying only lip service to the target language being the language of instruction.

1. If you teach in a bilingual class or in a class in which many students share the same first language, how do you monitor use of first versus target language?

_____

_____

2. What strategies do you use consistently to ensure that the target language is the language of instruction?

_____

_____

168

3. Do you use the shared language to explain the rationale or procedures for an activity if these cannot be explained in the target language?   Yes ❏   No ❏

4. What classroom language (e.g., vocabulary used in instructions) do you teach and use consistently to increase use of the target language?

_____

_____

5. Which of the following techniques do you use to ensure student comprehension when delivering instructions in the target language?

— I speak slowly.
— I repeat and rephrase.
— I rely heavily on gestures and body language.
— I use props and visual aids.
— I check for comprehension as exhibited through student responses more often than I otherwise might.
— Other: _____

6. What basic survival expressions in the target language do you teach and have students use regularly? Do you teach greetings, small talk, etc., to facilitate interaction in the target language?

_____

_____

7. When do you use the shared language?

_____

_____

8. Video- or audiotape your class and monitor the use of first and target languages. Is there an appropriate balance? Are you using the shared language more than you should?

_____

_____

Task 6

If you teach in a bilingual class or if many of your students share a common language, conduct an experiment and make your students part of it. For one teaching day or lesson, no one is allowed to use a single word of any language other than the language being taught. Explain to students the day before that, in order to make yourselves understood, you will all have to use all possible communication strategies, and that anyone who uses the shared language (including yourself) has to pay a "fine." (This may be pencils, pens, erasers, etc.—anything that will not compromise having fun with the experiment.) If possible, record the class and watch or listen to the tape the next day so that both you and the students can see and hear the communication that went on.

1. What conclusions do you draw from the experiment?

_____

_____

2. Identify the communication strategies you and your students adopted. Could these strategies be used in your class on a regular basis?

_____

_____

Task 7

We have all experienced group activities that worked wonders but also at least a few that failed either because they were not conducted effectively or because our expectations were unrealistic. When a teacher explains what needs to be discussed and then leaves students on their own, for example, not much communication is likely to occur. Successful communicative activities must be planned, and precommunicative work needs to lay the groundwork with necessary language elements and instructions. The teacher must then monitor the activity closely and continually, encouraging communication throughout. Guided discussions are structured so that even shy or withdrawn students have a turn to take part, and everyone's opinion is recorded.

It should also be noted that discussion should not be used early in a program, when students do not know each other well. As explained in Bassano and Christison's chapter in Michael Long and Jack Richards' *Methodology in TESOL*, our expectations are often unrealistic: "We put a room full of strangers into a circle and we expect them to act as close friends, before they even know or trust each other" (p. 202).

1. What do you do once your students have started working in groups? How do you make sure that communicative activities do not turn into monologues or silence?

_____

_____

2. Conduct a discussion as a group activity in your class and evaluate it against the points mentioned above.

_____

_____

11. Questions and Responses

A great deal of interaction in the classroom is initiated through questions and answers. The quality of our questions and how we ask them profoundly affects the quality of student responses and ensuing discussion. Similarly, the way we respond to our students' questions—and the way they respond to ours—has a tremendous impact on the classroom atmosphere and student learning.

Teacher Questions

Few aspects of teaching have been the focus of as much attention and research as teacher questions. Indeed, knowing how and when to ask appropriate questions is considered among our most important skills. With the introduction of video- and audiotaping in the classroom, practically every teacher can (and should) examine with considerable objectivity this aspect of his or her teaching. The results of self-evaluation in this area can be dramatic, since even minor changes in questioning techniques can have very positive effects.

Task 1

Analyze the types of questions you ask.

1. Do you try to ask questions that require more than a one- or two-word response?

Yes, deliberately ❑   No, not consciously ❑

2. How often do you ask thought-provoking questions in which students are challenged to think about and express their opinions?

Often ❑   Sometimes ❑   Rarely ❑   Never ❑

3. How often do you ask questions aimed at determining if students understand your lesson or a text?

Often ❑   Sometimes ❑   Rarely ❑   Never ❑

4. Do you know what the answers will be before you ask the question?

Always ❑ Often ❑ Sometimes ❑ Rarely ❑ Never ❑

5. Do you ask questions that anticipate responses from more than one student (e.g., "Who's seen the movie version of this play? What did you all think of it?") and then allow time for answers and discussion?

Always ❑ Often ❑ Sometimes ❑ Rarely ❑ Never ❑

6. Do you use students' responses to diagnose the areas within the subject matter that may require more work?

Always ❑ Often ❑ Sometimes ❑ Rarely ❑ Never ❑

Task 2

Try to examine different types of questions you use and their benefits for different students in various lessons. While working on your next lesson plan, write down ten questions you plan to ask. After the lesson, refer to the list to determine whether you actually asked the questions and, if so, consider the effect your questioning had. (If possible, video- or audiotape the lesson so that your answers will be more objective and accurate.)

1. List your questions.

_____   _____

_____   _____

_____   _____

_____   _____

_____   _____

2. What types of questions are they? Enter the appropriate number for each category.

Yes-or-no questions:

Short-answer questions:

Long-answer questions:

3. How much time did your students need to respond to your questions?

_____

_____

4. Were your questions clearly worded?

Yes ❑ No ❑

5. Were your questions worded to encourage student response?

Yes ❑ No ❑

6. Were your questions phrased in the sort of language you would use outside of the classroom? Why or why not?

_____

_____

7. Analyze a question your students had trouble with. What factors made that question challenging?

_____

_____

8. Do you think your questioning skills could be improved? If so, how will you go about improving them?

_____

_____

_____

_____

Task 3

In "Classroom Foreigner Talk Discourse," Michael Long and Charlene Sato describe studies they conducted on the kinds of questions used both in school (specifically in ESL classrooms) and in "real life." They distinguished between *display* questions (those whose answers are known to the questioner) and *referential* questions (those whose answers are unknown to all parties). The language teachers were found to ask significantly more display questions than referential ones in the classroom, while in nonschool settings, virtually no display questions were asked. This finding, we feel, may have relevance to teachers across subject disciplines.

Clearly, when we ask referential questions in the classroom we stand a greater chance of prompting real-life interaction among students. Such questions also generally result in more complex, lengthy answers. Display questions, however, also have an important role to play. One challenge of teaching children or teenagers lies in holding their attention when we need to explain new content. Display questions can be used during explanation as a follow-up to the key points being presented. This makes students focus on what is being explained in anticipation of being questioned, which may help establish a lively rhythm in this phase of the lesson.

1. Of the questions you listed in Task 2, how many are display and how many referential?

Display questions: Referential questions:

2. Do the numbers confirm Long and Sato's finding?

_____

_____

3. For what purposes do you use display questions in your lessons?

_____

_____

Task 4

Research has indicated that we use significantly more imperatives and statements—and fewer questions—in the classroom than we do in our real-life interactions (Nunan & Lamb, 1996). Also, we use more questions that encourage only a short response.

1. Video- or audiotape a lesson. Review the tape, and select a segment during which you interact with your students. Count the number of imperatives, statements, and yes-no or short-answer questions you use.

Imperatives   Statements   Yes-no/short-answer questions

2. Evaluate the quality of interaction in this segment. Do you think there is anything that needs to be changed? Would the interaction have been significantly improved if you had asked different questions?

_____

_____

3. In an upcoming lesson, try to use more referential questions. What do you notice?

_____

_____

Common Errors

A mistake is a superb teacher of success.
JOHNNETTA B. COLE, *DREAM THE BOLDEST DREAMS*

It would obviously be impossible to write down all the questions you plan to ask in a lesson and to analyze the implications of each one. The type of questions and the way they are asked often depends on how the lesson unfolds—on the way students respond and the unplanned things that happen. We also need to take into consideration that teaching is an "on-line" process, and during a lesson we are usually thinking more about content than about questions. Thus, errors in questioning are inevitable. Consider the following scenarios:

- An elementary school teacher followed up each of her questions with a series of three or four more questions intended to clarify and help students understand the initial question. She was puzzled by the fact that she often did not get the responses she expected.
- An ESL teacher asked his students, "What do you think about the police in this area?" Without pausing, he continued, "How did you like the policeman who was a guest speaker here? Was he nice? Yes? No?" The students looked on in confusion.
- On Monday morning, a middle school teacher entered his class and, without focusing on anyone in particular, said, "How was your weekend? Was it busy? Nice? Or busy and nice, 'cause sometimes being busy can be nice?" He was met by silence.

If you had been a student in one of these classes, how would you have reacted? In the first instance, the teacher failed to realize that students were responding to the question they held in memory—that is, the last one. And since this was much more focused and specific than the initial "main" question, the students' responses were not what the teacher had hoped. In the second case, the teacher gave his students no time to process the questions he asked, which were a jumble of the long-, short-, and one-word–answer type. And in the third, the teacher seemed to be rambling, perhaps out of nervousness at the possibility of conversational silence.

Task 1

The teachers described above would have benefited from taping and analyzing question-answer portions of their interaction with students. If you have access to recording equipment, make a tape and transcribe a segment of questions and answers. If this is not possible, try to complete this task after careful reflection on how questioning works with your students.

1. In your last few lessons, how often did you make the following errors in questioning?

	Often	Sometimes	Never
I did not give students enough time to process questions, but started assisting them right away.			
I looked at one student when I asked a question, then confused him or her by calling on someone else to answer.			
I asked questions that were too easy, and students put no effort into their responses.			
I asked questions that students did not understand, so I had to reword them.			
I asked and answered my own rhetorical questions.			
My questions were inappropriate (e.g., they asked for too much personal disclosure).			
I asked some students noticeably more questions than others.			
I posed sequential questions, giving students inadequate time to process each of them and no reason to respond.			

2. From a student's perspective, which of the above do you think is the worst-case scenario? Why?

_____

_____

3. How do you think students feel about rhetorical questions? How do you think you would react to them if you were a student?

_____

_____

4. In your analysis of your questioning, what strengths have been revealed?

_____

_____

176

Student Participation and Responses

We have all conducted or observed classes where students spend most of their time in silence, speaking only when called on, where a few outspoken students dominate, or where everyone speaks at once. Teachers' skills in questioning can improve these sorts of classroom atmospheres and have a profound effect on the quality of student responses.

 Task 1

Try to monitor which students are responding to your questions. In your next lesson, use an existing class list and cross off the names of any students who are absent. As you conduct the lesson, place a checkmark next to the names of students who respond to your questions or prompts. (You can use the same technique while playing back a tape of a previously recorded lesson.)

1. Did you call on any students more often than others?

Yes ❑   No ❑

2. Did all students get equal amounts of your attention?

Yes ❑   No ❑

3. Did you neglect any of your students?

Yes ❑   No ❑

4. If yes, whom? Why?

_____

_____

5. How did you demonstrate interest in your students' responses?

_____

_____

6. Did any students not participate at all? If so, why do you think this was the case?

_____

_____

7. Have any patterns surfaced? Are you satisfied with them? If not, what could you change?

_____

_____

Task 2

Try to identify the factors that influence decisions about who will respond to your questions.

1. What approach do you take?

	Always	Sometimes	Rarely	Never
I try to pick up my students' signals and ask only those who want to respond.				
I ask students to raise their hands.				
I call on students at random.				
I call names according to a previously prepared plan.				
Learners respond following their seating pattern.				
Other: _____				

2. What is the rationale behind your usual approach?

_____

_____

3. As a follow-up, create a survey with the above-listed options for your students, to determine their preferences.

Task 3

In every class, there are students who are noisier and more talkative than others. They tend to "grab the microphone" and monopolize interaction. Novices beware! Finding effective ways of cutting down these students' talk time can be difficult, but it is essential to do so in order to ensure that all students get a chance to take part.

1. One possibility is to reword what a dominating student says, let him or her know that you appreciate the input, and then state directly that you would like to find out what other students think about the issue. Can you think of other approaches?

_____

_____

2. Have you encountered similar situations? What approach did you take? Was it effective?

_____

_____

Task 4

Besides talkative students, every class includes learners with low self-esteem. Teachers must make special, but sensitive, efforts to draw these students into discussion.

1. Which of the following do you do to make insecure students feel comfortable while participating in class?

— I ask questions that require different levels of proficiency to ensure that shy or lower level students can experience success.
— I always offer praise and encouragement, even if performance is lacking.
— I talk to those students individually before or after class to offer encouragement.
— I monitor grouping patterns to ensure that shy students are not "dwarfed" by outgoing and noisy ones.
— Other: _____

2. Are you content with the way you are dealing with shy students?

Yes ❑   To some extent ❑   There's room for improvement ❑

Wait Time and Listening

In order to be effective communicators, we need to have good listening skills. Being a good listener in the classroom implies two things: giving students enough "wait time" to process your questions, and displaying willingness to hear what they have to say. Obviously, students cannot express themselves if we are not patient and attentive ourselves.

Task 1

Reviewing a video- or audiotape of a few of your lessons may help you answer the following questions. If this is not an option, try to recall how you handled aspects of waiting and listening in your last few lessons.

1. How much time do you usually wait for a response to a yes-no question before you help the student or ask someone else?

1 second   2 seconds   3 or more seconds

2. How much time do you usually wait for the response to an open-ended question before you help the student or ask someone else?

1 second   2 seconds   3 or more seconds

3. Once a student has answered, how much time do you usually wait before posing another question?

1 second   2 seconds   3 or more seconds

4. If your response to any of the three preceding questions was "1 second," try to prolong the wait time during one of your next lessons. Did it have an effect? If so, describe it.

_____

_____

5. In a research report, Mary Budd Rowe indicates that "The length of student responses increases between 300% and 700%, in some cases more" if wait time is 3 seconds or longer (p. 44). Do you think this would be worth trying in your classes? How relevant do you feel this is?

_____

_____

Student Questions

If real learning is to take place, students must be able to ask for explanations, clarification, or repetition. This communication skill is even more crucial outside the classroom. We should therefore show students that we value their questions by encouraging them to ask and by responding appropriately.

Task 1

Responding to students' questions is much more complex than may be assumed. The approach we probably should be taking is "situational"—that is, the way we react should be based on an assessment of the best course of action for a particular situation. Consider the following scenario:

A student in an adult ESL class expressed dissatisfaction with the way a new teacher responded to questions. In an obvious attempt to promote interaction and student talk, the teacher directed all questions to other learners and asked them to provide explanations. The problem for this student was that her questions about vocabulary items often had more to do with pronunciation than with meaning or use. The teacher did not repeat answers himself, so the only model of pronunciation the student had was provided by the other non-native speakers in the class. This simple-to-remedy breakdown in communication was a source of considerable frustration for the student—and it was probably frustrating for the teacher, too, since he was picking up the student's signals.

1. What do you usually do when a student asks for clarification?

— I repeat the question and address it.
— I address the question by conversing with that student only.
— I repeat the question and ask whether anyone in class can provide the answer.
— I elicit answers from other students and repeat or rephrase them.
— Other: _____

It depends on: _____

2. Where are you positioned when you answer questions?

I stand next to the student who asked the question.
I move to a spot in the classroom where everyone can see me.
It depends on: _____

3. Do you think some of these options make a difference? Why?

_____

_____

4. How do you make sure that students are satisfied with your handling of questions?

_____

_____

Task 2

Students often ask questions we are unable to answer, and sometimes they challenge the answers we do give. Teachers are often puzzled about what to do in such situations, and some inexperienced teachers or those lacking in self-confidence try to come up with any response they can, even if they are not certain that it is correct.

1. What do you think is the best course of action when a student asks a question a teacher does not know how to answer?

— Teachers should admit that they don't know the answer.
— Teachers should tell their students that they don't know but will find out.
— Teachers should tell their students that they don't know but will find out, and should do so as soon as possible.
— Teachers should come up with an answer to avoid "losing face."
— Teachers should pretend they have not heard the question or should ignore it.
— Other: _____

2. What is your own usual reaction in this situation? Does it match what you consider to be the best course? Why or why not?

_____

_____

3. In a chapter in *The Craft of Teaching Adults*, his book edited with Thelma Barer-Stein, James Draper reports the words of a teacher who was asked about feelings associated with not always being able to respond to students' questions: "I am not ashamed if I do not know the answer to every question. I want the students to see that I am human and I don't expect myself, or others, to

'know it all.' What is important is that we collectively know how to go about finding the answer." Do you agree with this strategy?

_____

_____

Task 3

Our students' questions and comments can take our lessons in entirely unexpected directions. By adopting a positive approach to unexpected developments, we can turn them into learning experiences; if our attitude is negative, they cause nothing but stress and frustration. The next time something unexpected happens in your class, try to monitor how you react and what you do.

1. Describe the situation:

_____

_____

2. What did you do? How do you feel about the way you dealt with the event?

_____

_____

3. In general, how do you account for spontaneous instruction? What is your rationale?

_____

_____

Task 4

The way students respond in class discussions can give us ideas for new teaching directions or minilessons on particular topics. We should try to be attentive to students' needs and interests, even if they are expressed in unplanned ways.

1. To what extent do you incorporate flexibility into your lesson plans?

_____

_____

2. Analyze a videotape of your teaching. How did you make the most of unplanned situations?

_____

_____

Special Considerations for the Language Teacher

In the language-teaching context, questions take on an added dimension. Part of interaction in these classrooms centers on questioning in order to clarify the language used in instruction.

Task 1

We can use a number of strategies to teach students how to ask questions:

- directly teaching basic survival questions and expressions (e.g., "Can you repeat that, please?" "How do you spell that?"), posting them around the room and referring to them often;
- highlighting the focused-repetition technique in which the known part of a statement is repeated to highlight the unknown (e.g., "Mary had that book." "Mary had what?");
- audiotaping student interaction and analyzing errors;
- modeling exchanges;
- teaching the "mechanics" of question formation (the use of auxiliary words and word order);
- facilitating the use of clarification questions in pair and group work and providing students with ample practice;
- teaching proper body language to indicate lack of comprehension;
- rewarding students for asking clarification questions; and
- facilitating self- and peer correction through a variety of techniques.

1. Which of the above techniques do you use?

_____

_____

2. Try one of the techniques you don't use regularly. Does it have any effect on your students?

_____

_____

3. Do you use other ways of facilitating your students' questions?

_____

_____

Task 2

During a class I [Vesna] conducted, my adult students were listening to a caller on a phone-in radio show. One of the students asked for clarification. Following is a partial transcript of my tape of that class:

Student 1: Now, she wanted to go and sue him to court, and her father said, "No"?
Or...?
Me: She didn't clearly say that....
Student 2: (joining in) She's in doubt.
Me: She never mentioned that. She just doesn't know what to do about it....
Student 2: She doubts....
Me: She has doubts...doubts about what to do or whether she should do anything at all....

It was only when I started transcribing the tape and tried to figure out who said what first that I realized the second student knew the answer and was trying to express it all the while I was talking. I did not have to be the provider of the correct response—my student could have done it.

How do you encourage students to answer one another's questions? Do you check whether your students can provide the responses instead of you?

_____

_____

Task 3

Students need to learn not only how to ask questions in the target language, but how to respond to them as a native speaker might. In *The Context of Language Teaching*, Jack Richards describes research that revealed that native English speakers usually reply to a yes-or-no question not with "yes" or "no," but rather by providing a response that makes it clear whether the question has been answered "positively, negatively, or in some other way" (p. 96). In classrooms, however, teachers often encourage students to respond with "yes" or "no," followed by an auxiliary verb (e.g., "Do you like sports?" "Yes, I do."). Richards claims that because this is not typical of real language use, it is of no value to students.

1. Try to monitor how native speakers respond to questions. Do you notice what Richards reports?

Yes ❑   No ❑   To some extent ❑

2. What do you think about Richards' statement regarding the value of yes-or-no questions in relation to the response patterns you teach?

_____

_____

12. Feedback and Correction

What do you do in response to your students' performance? Do you smile, look serious, or maybe frown and shake your head? Do you offer lavish praise? Do you chastise students for forgetting a previous lesson or punish by assigning a bad grade? Do you acknowledge good responses with a nod or dismiss them with a shrug, evaluate them or ignore them altogether? All of these options fall into the category of feedback.

Most often feedback is provided orally or in writing, but it can also be expressed in nonverbal forms through body language, gestures, or facial expressions. It can be negative or positive, and can relate to aspects of either the content or form of a student's production or performance. If that production or performance is lacking in some way, the teacher's feedback may be offered as *correction*.

This chapter explores various effective techniques for giving feedback and correction and highlights how teachers go about making appropriate choices. We also discuss common problems in this area.

Positive and Negative Feedback

For we, which now behold these present days,
Have eyes to wonder, but lack tongues to praise.
WILLIAM SHAKESPEARE, SONNET CVI

Picture this scenario: You volunteer to do a special task for your school principal. In order to complete it, you have to put in considerable effort and work extra hours. When it is finished, you are certain you have done an excellent job. Full of enthusiasm, you stop by the principal's office with expectations that your work will be well received. Instead, she barely acknowledges it, much less offers you credit or praise.

Lack of recognition for hard work hurts immensely and has a highly negative influence on motivation. Unfortunately, it can be experienced anywhere. To ensure that it does not occur in your own classroom, consider how you offer feedback by completing the following tasks.

Task 1

How do you provide feedback for both correct and incorrect responses? Your answers to the following questions will be more accurate and objective if you are able to videotape a few lessons and complete this task after watching the tapes.

1. Note in point form several instances of feedback you offered in response to both correct (column 1) and incorrect (column 3) responses from students (e.g., nodded and said, "Well done!"; shook my head, saying, "Anyone else?"). Rate each action by entering a numeral from 1 (not effective) to 5 (very effective) in the adjacent column.

Feedback to correct response	Rating	Feedback to incorrect response	Rating

2. Does one column contain considerably more entries or do you have a good balance? If one is longer, why do you think this is the case?

_____

_____

3. For each of the following examples of corrective feedback, try to come up with wording that might be more effective or appropriate.

Example	Your wording
No, that's not correct.	
Not exactly.	
No.... Does someone else have a better answer?	
Is that your answer?	
You'd better think again.	
Pardon? What did you just say?	

4. Corrective feedback starting with the word "No" may serve only to create barriers, especially for adult learners or students with low self-esteem. Discuss the preceding list of examples with your students. What wording do they prefer?

_____

_____

5. Can you think of ways that your feedback techniques could be made more effective?

_____

_____

_____

_____

Task 2

1. What type of oral feedback do you offer most often?

Feedback on content (what is said or written) ❏   Feedback on form (how it is said or written) ❏

2. When you offer feedback, do you give the student an opportunity to use that feedback to improve performance? If so, how?

_____

_____

3. Rank order the type of feedback you provide, according to frequency.

Feedback on writing skills   Feedback on speaking skills
Feedback on listening comprehension   Feedback on reading comprehension
Feedback on language structures used   Feedback on vocabulary use
Feedback on class participation   Feedback on behavior
Feedback on progress   Feedback on use of strategies that have been
Feedback on mistakes   taught
Feedback on content learned   Feedback on test results
Other: _____

4. Is there any type of feedback listed above that you never or hardly ever provide? If so, why?

_____

_____

5. Try to recall your own experience as a student. How often were you praised by your teachers? When and how were you criticized? How did these occurrences make you feel? What conclusions can you draw for your own teaching situation?

_____

_____

Task 3

While positive feedback motivates students and improves performance, too much negative feedback or a complete lack of feedback can raise barriers to learning. Experienced teachers seem to be able to balance positive and negative feedback, and can see students' accomplishments even when they are obscured by errors. They have a sixth sense for providing corrective feedback in a manner that does not discourage students but rather helps them see that they can learn from mistakes.

1. What do you do when offering oral feedback to your students?

I provide positive feedback by praising and acknowledging students' performance, progress, hard work, commitment, etc.
Yes ❑   No ❑   Sometimes ❑

I acknowledge students' contributions to my class and feedback related to my teaching that they provide.
Yes ❑   No ❑   Sometimes ❑

I offer constructive criticism, ensuring that I begin on a positive note.
Yes ❑   No ❑   Sometimes ❑

I make generalized criticisms.
Yes ❑   No ❑   Sometimes ❑

I make blanket statements.
Yes ❑   No ❑   Sometimes ❑

I react negatively.
Yes ❑   No ❑   Sometimes ❑

2. Which of these teacher behaviors did you find most irritating when you were a student?

_____

_____

Task 4

Providing students with well-balanced and effective written feedback is a real art. To find out what is involved and to assess your mastery, photocopy some random samples of student work that you have evaluated with written comments. (Since we all seem to see things more objectively after some time has passed, it is a good idea to select assignments you graded at least ten days previously.) Analyze the wording of your comments and the manner in which the feedback was provided. Also, check if you made any mistakes in your corrections.

Your comment/feedback	Could it have been worded differently? How?

Task 5

For beginning writers and second- or foreign-language learners, it is imperative that we offer written corrective feedback on written assignments. If you teach such a group, reflect on the written feedback you provide.

1. What do you correct?

— All mistakes
— Selected mistakes
— It depends on: _____

2. What criteria do you use to determine what and how much to correct?

— Students' level of proficiency
— Stage in the course (beginning, middle, or end)
— Course goals (creative writing, advanced language learning, etc.)
— Students' goals
— Other: _____

3. Do you provide corrections or simply cross out errors?

_____

_____

4. Do you provide a balance of encouragement and correction, or do you tend to focus more on either positive or negative feedback?

_____

_____

5. Do you discuss your feedback with students? Why or why not?

_____

_____

6. Do you summarize feedback for individual students and provide suggestions related to aspects of their writing they need to improve?

_____

_____

7. How do you indicate that a whole sentence or passage needs to be changed?

_____

_____

8. Many language teachers use a numbering system to indicate error type—1, for example, might mean incorrect tense, and 2 might indicate a spelling mistake. Have you ever tried this? If so, what is your system? If not, do any of your colleagues use a similar system, and could you share or adapt theirs? Might such an approach be useful?

_____

_____

Correction

To err is human... (and correction should be done humanely).

When it comes to correction, it is important that teachers recognize the difference between an "error" and a "mistake." In an article in the *ELT Journal*, Keith Johnson repeats Corder's distinction between *errors* that result when students have not yet acquired the knowledge needed to respond and *mistakes* that arise when students have the required knowledge but lack the ability to process it. In a language class, for example, a student might correctly complete a drill exercise on the present perfect tense, but may make mistakes with the same structures when interacting less formally with classmates.

If we follow this distinction, it seems logical to conclude that correcting students' errors is not terribly worthwhile, since they occur because students do not have the necessary knowledge. As

190

long as the teacher knows that at some point the student will be taught the "missing pieces," errors may be temporarily dismissed. Monitoring of student errors should continue, however, since this can serve as an important guide for program planning and curriculum design.

What remains as the focus of our attention, then, is correction of mistakes. Johnson suggests that feedback of this type has an important function in the classroom: "The sequence of events, in this case, is not learn ➡ perform, but learn ➡ perform ➡ learn. This sequence correctly suggests that when we speak about feedback, we are speaking about something that potentially contributes to the learning process" (1988, p. 90).

Task 1

1. Do you correct your students' errors, mistakes, or both?

_____

_____

2. Do you monitor student errors to provide information for course planning?

_____

_____

3. To observe what and how you correct, record a few lessons. Play back the tape and focus on segments in which you offer feedback. Note the number of each type of correction you provide.

Mistake correction   Error correction

4. Analyze the instances of error correction. What was your rationale?

_____

_____

Task 2

We all have had students at two extremes in our classes: the perfectionist who passes all tests with flying colors but hardly says a word, and the nonstop babbler who appears not at all troubled by his or her frequent mistakes and seems to feel no need to correct them. Keith Johnson identifies four prerequisites necessary before students can correct their mistakes:

- the desire or need to eradicate the mistake;
- an internal representation of the correct behavior;
- a realization that the performance given is flawed; and
- an opportunity to practice in real conditions (1988, p. 91).

1. During a lesson, monitor two students (or, better yet, watch a videorecording and focus on two students), and then analyze their mistakes and their own attitudes toward them.

	Student	Student
Does the student see the need to correct the mistake?		
Does the student possess the knowledge necessary to eradicate the mistake?		
Is the student aware that a mistake was made?		
Is the student given the opportunity to perform the task again, without the mistake?		
How does the student feel about his or her mistakes?		

2. What conclusions can you draw? How true of your students are Johnson's views on the four prerequisites?

_____

_____

Task 3

Hoping to improve his lessons, a teacher asked his group of adult students to think about what in his teaching practice they would like to see altered. Students dropped their suggestions into a box on the teacher's desk. One of the notes read, "Please always tell me when I'm wrong," and two others offered similar comments. The next day the teacher told the students that he would like to respond to their request, and that during the lesson's first activity he would attempt to correct anything and everything. The activity began, and the teacher interrupted students each time they made mistakes or errors. Students soon became unable to finish their thoughts, and they started getting frustrated.

As the time allotted for the activity elapsed, the teacher announced that it would take an additional 90 minutes to do what was planned. He then engaged students in a discussion of the type of correction he had been offering, and it became obvious that much of it related to students' lack of knowledge of the very material the lesson was designed to cover. He then referred students to the course outline so that they would see that this material had been included in it and would be covered.

1. If you were a student in this class, how would you feel about the teacher's experiment in correction?

_____

_____

2. What do you as a teacher think about the method described?

_____

_____

3. What message was conveyed to these students?

_____

_____

4. If your students made a similar request, how would you deal with it?

_____

_____

Task 4

In the *Self-Directed Teacher*, Nunan and Lamb write as follows:

> The answer to the question of when a teacher should correct a student's error must be "it depends." In many contexts, when the focus is on meaning, it is probably inappropriate to interrupt the flow of interaction. In these situations, the teacher can make a note of the errors for follow-up treatment later. (Of course, if the error interferes with communication, then the teacher may have to intervene.) In other contexts, when the focus is on form, then the teacher might well interrupt before the students have finished their turn.

(Note that Nunan and Lamb do not adhere to Corder's distinction between *error* and *mistake*.)

Finding a good balance in correction can be difficult. After watching her correction techniques on a few videos, an ESL teacher of adults wrote the following:

> Another courageous student came forward with a one-sentence story of what happened to her last week. I responded to her mistake by repeating her sentence and correcting the incorrectly used verb. Being a motivated student, she repeated it, obviously trying to remember it, and continued with her story. This seems to be an example of a good strategy on behalf of both the teacher and the student. The correction was possible because the utterance was short. I find it a real challenge, however, when students talk in longer stretches, and I do not want to interrupt them, as everyone in class can still understand them regardless of the errors or mistakes made....

1. Select an upcoming activity you are planning and identify whether it focuses on form or content. What type of mistakes or errors will you correct?

_____

_____

2. When will you offer correction?

— Immediately, by interrupting the student
— Immediately, by indicating the mistake to the student nonverbally
— At the conclusion of the activity
— In a subsequent lesson, after I have a chance to analyze the types of errors and mistakes

3. Conduct the activity. Did thinking through your techniques for offering correction change the way it proceeded?

_____

_____

Task 5

1. Indicate the percentage of time you usually use each of the following techniques for offering correction.

— I react to all mistakes immediately by interrupting. ____%
— I correct mistakes immediately and later test how effective the correction technique was. ____%
— Even though I notice mistakes, I do not react immediately. ____%
— I allow students to finish their thoughts, and then I correct the mistake. ____%
— I note the common mistakes and use this as a basis for teaching during the next couple of lessons. ____%
— I note a student's mistakes and then work with that student later, on a one-to-one basis. ____%
— I indicate nonverbally that something was incorrect, hoping that the student will get the message. ____%
— I try to indicate verbally to the student that a mistake has been made and encourage the student to come up with a correction, offering help if necessary. ____%
— I ask other students if they can help. ____%
— I rephrase what the student said, correcting the mistake by example. ____%
— I tape students during activities and analyze mistakes with them during playback. ____%
— Other: _____ %

2. Do you ever discuss with your students the rationale for your correction techniques?

_____

_____

3. If you were a student and made a mistake or error, which of the options in question 1 would you like your teacher to use when correcting you? Why?

_____

_____

4. Which of the options would you find annoying?

_____

_____

5. If possible, tape a few lessons and analyze segments in which you offer corrections. Note what you did, your rationale, how students responded, and whether the technique was effective. Is there any room for improvement?

_____

_____

_____

_____

Task 6

It may be helpful for teachers to determine what type of correction their students prefer. Students may ask to have all errors corrected (as in the scenario described in Task 3) or only some; they may say they prefer being prompted, given choices, or simply told that an error had been made. They may respond well to verbal, nonverbal, or written correction.

Create a survey to determine your students' preferences with regard to the method of correction, types of mistakes that should be corrected, and the frequency of correction. What are the results?

_____

_____

Task 7

Peer correction can extend teacher correction, increasing student involvement in the process. We must keep in mind, however, that students' response to peer correction has a cultural dimension. In some contexts, correction from a peer may be considered by students as intrusive, impolite, and "pushy" on the part of the giver and embarrassing to the recipient.

I [Hanna] once taught a high school ESL class in which the students were all Korean. They were reluctant to engage in peer correction, and when it was offered, they disregarded it. I found that when the students were provided with a prescribed sequence of steps for peer correction, they were able to correct more because they viewed the process as a teacher-initiated exercise. They also came to see that it contributed to their own learning.

For example, as part of the process approach to writing, I asked students to correct one another's drafts and provided the following guidelines:

- Step 1—read your partner's story to see if every sentence starts with a capital letter and ends with a full stop.
- Step 2—read the story to see if every sentence has a subject and a verb.
- Step 3—read the story to see if the subject agrees with the verb.
- Step 4—read the story to see if every verb is in the proper tense.

195

1. Have you ever tried peer correction? If so, was it successful? If not, do you think it could benefit your students?

_____

_____

2. Have you used a technique such as the one described? If so, what were the steps? If not, would it be worth trying?

_____

_____

13. Motivation and Attitude

The role of motivation in both learning and teaching cannot be overestimated. In *Teaching by Principles*, H. Douglas Brown presents a comprehensive overview of research in this area and offers a definition of *motivation* as "the extent to which you make choices about a) goals to pursue and b) the effort you will devote to that pursuit" (p. 32).

There have been many attempts to study and classify the factors involved in motivation. For some time a distinction between "integrative" and "instrumental" motivation enjoyed wide popularity—the former being motivation spurred by a need and desire to integrate and identify with a community and the latter arising from a desire to acquire skills or knowledge to use as a tool for achieving other goals. Integrative motivation was thought to be somewhat stronger and longer lasting, though studies in this area have proved quite inconclusive.

Another popular division is between "intrinsic" motivation that stems from a desire to fulfill personal needs, goals, or ambitions without the promise of a specific reward and "extrinsic" motivation that comes from the desire to obtain such rewards. Here, intrinsic motivation is thought to be the more powerful.

Common sense supports the idea that accomplishment is one of the best motivators. When we have tangible evidence that we are achieving goals or are effective in what we are doing, motivation increases and is sustained over periods of time. Failure, on the other hand, is a negative experience that often results in loss of motivation. In education, these ideas hold true for both students and teachers. If teachers are content with the results of their work, they will embrace their next assignment with more enthusiasm and greater motivation. Similarly, students who experience success in school will be more eager to participate and expand their knowledge. Needless to say, the lack of results turns a course into a burden for both teachers and students.

This chapter focuses on student and teacher motivation from a broad and practical point of view rather than theoretical one, in an attempt to assist readers in identifying teacher and learner qualities and how they contribute to relationships in the classroom.

Student Motivation

It seems logical to see motivation as a spectrum of complex, varied, and individualized factors. Generally, however, we might describe a motivated student as one who is

- willing to engage in all learning tasks;

197

- interested in all aspects of the subject matter;
- eager to cooperate with the teacher and classmates;
- ready to invest energy in the assigned tasks;
- willing to pursue independent learning outside of class;
- able to stay on task;
- willing to encourage classmates to work conscientiously;
- ready to provide suggestions on how the program could be improved; and
- able to ask relevant questions about the content being taught.

Task 1

1. Which of the following factors do you think is most important for learning?

Hard work
Aptitude
Persistence
Motivation
Other: _____

2. If a learner lacks one of the factors listed above, can she or he compensate with another? If so, can you think of any students whose cases illustrate this point?

Student's name	Factor missing	Compensating factor
_____	_____	_____
_____	_____	_____
_____	_____	_____
_____	_____	_____
_____	_____	_____

3. Rank order the descriptors that provide the most relevant conclusion to the following statement: "In order to learn best, students need to be...."

relaxed	motivated	rested
hardworking	interested	comfortable
patient	involved	other: _____

4. How do you capitalize on these qualities among your learners?

_____

_____

Task 2

If students have satisfying learning experiences, that feeling of satisfaction and accomplishment motivates them to study further. One of our roles, therefore, is to ensure that initial learning experiences are as positive as possible.

1. Provide an example for each of the ways you have enhanced student motivation in recent lessons.

Way of enhancing motivation	Example
I set objectives that are relevant to students' personal goals.	
I appeal to students' need and desire to explore and learn.	
I involve students in selecting activities, materials, and tasks.	
I appeal to students' interests.	
I offer students a lot of positive feedback and encouragement.	
I design tasks that enable learners to experience a sense of accomplishment.	
I match tasks to the proficiency levels of individual students.	
Other: _____	

2. Monitor student motivation during your next week of teaching. For each of the activities you plan, rate the level of motivation you expect on a scale from 1 (low) to 5 (high). After the activity is complete, rate the actual level of motivation you observed.

Activity	Expected motivation	Actual motivation	Conclusions
_____	_____	_____	_____
_____	_____	_____	_____
_____	_____	_____	_____
_____	_____	_____	_____
_____	_____	_____	_____

Activity	Expected motivation	Actual motivation	Conclusions
_____ _____	_____ _____	_____ _____	_____ _____

3. Select an activity for which the expected and actual levels of motivation differed significantly. Survey your students on their feelings about the activity.

— Did they understand its purpose?
— Did they find it useful?
— Was it aimed at the appropriate proficiency level?
— Did they feel the timing for the activity was reasonable?
— Was it relevant to their circumstances and goals?
— Did they recognize it as having real-world significance?
— Did they enjoy working on the task?

4. Analyze students' answers to see if they suggest factors that may have influenced their level of motivation. What conclusions can you draw?

_____

_____

Task 3

1. The factors that motivate students are quite personal. What have you been able to find out about these factors for your current group of students?

_____

_____

2. Identify one of your students who lacks motivation, and try to determine what could be done to alter the situation.

Student's name: _____

Reasons for lack of motivation (if known):

_____

_____

Course of action:

_____

_____

Task 4

Inquiring about students' interests, hobbies, leisure activities, and goals has a twofold advantage: it shows your genuine interest in your students, and it can serve as a basis for planning future activities. If we build programs around materials and topics of interest to our students, we can capitalize on the increased motivation that is likely to result.

How much do you know about your students? Create a chart to list personal details for each student, under headings such as "Interests," "Hobbies/Leisure activities," and "Goals." Gather information to complete the chart as you monitor classroom communication or interview students, or pass the chart around and ask your students to fill it out. Do any common themes emerge? Could you design some upcoming activities to relate to these themes?

_____

_____

_____

_____

Task 5

Students are usually motivated at the outset of a course—they have high expectations, and the level of motivation they are able to sustain is directly proportional to the level at which their expectations come true. In elementary or high school settings where there is a "captive audience," decreases in motivation can lead to an unpleasant atmosphere for learning and teaching. With older students, there may also be an increase in lateness or truancy, particularly in programs where attendance and attitude are not part of evaluation. Motivational factors among adult students may have quite a serious impact on the fate of an entire course. If motivation is not maintained at a high enough level, students may simply drop out, occasionally in numbers sufficient to result in termination of the course.

What do you do to ensure that students' expectations are met to the largest possible degree? What effect do you feel this has on motivation?

_____

_____

_____

_____

Task 6

A noncredit course for adults is supposed to start at 9:00 a.m., but the only person in the room is the teacher. Slowly, students start strolling in and drifting to their places—there is no need to hurry, since the teacher is sitting at his desk, waiting for more students to arrive. After fifteen minutes, about half the students are present. The teacher looks up and says, "I am going to do some review for now, since so many people are absent." More students arrive during the review, with some sneaking in quietly while others greet everyone with a loud "Good morning!" The teacher stops the activity to respond to each greeting, and the class proceeds in a chopped-up rhythm for a few more minutes. Finally, at 9:30, the lesson for the day can begin. The teacher does not comment on the students' lateness, apparently happy that the class is now underway.

Do this task if you teach a noncredit program or a course in which student effort and attitude are not a component of evaluation.

1. How does the preceding scenario compare to your class?

_____

_____

2. What do you do to encourage attendance and punctuality?

	Always				Never
	5	4	3	2	1
I praise students who arrive on time.					
I take attendance regularly.					
I take attendance and also pass a record sheet around so that students can mark their own absences or late arrivals.					
I comment on lateness.					
I ensure that, in classes of adult students, everyone is aware of special considerations in place when childcare or work schedules conflict with punctuality and attendance.					
I try to find out the reasons for lateness or absenteeism.					
I "sum up" attendance periodically and convey the results to students.					
I am punctual and begin my lessons on time.					
I begin each class with an interesting activity.					
Other: _____					

3. Students may be more inclined to attend regularly if they know what they may be missing. How do you ensure that students are aware of upcoming course content?

— I provide students with a comprehensive list of long-range objectives.
— I refer to the parts of the program covered on a regular basis, relating them to current and upcoming material.
— I talk about future lesson plans and activities.
— Other: _____

4. If possible, videotape the first half-hour of your class for two or three days. Play back the tape and write a description of what happens when students arrive late. Is there room for change?

_____

_____

5. Devise an action plan of what you can do to increase student motivation and prevent lateness and absenteeism.

_____

_____

_____

_____

Teacher Qualities

> *And gladly wolde he lerne and gladly teche.*
> GEOFFREY CHAUCER, *THE CANTERBURY TALES*

Teacher qualities and traits are like genes: each teacher has a unique combination that sets him or her apart from all others. If you think back to your own teachers and compare their qualities, you will certainly agree with this statement. You will also agree that a teacher's qualities have a great deal to do with how motivated students are to do their best in class.

Task 1

Mary Torti, a teacher at St. Martha School in Toronto, asked a group of grade 7 and 8 students to read a list of traits that characterized "good" and "bad" teachers and to rank them according to their perceptions of teacher qualities. (The traits came from Luke Prodromou's list of qualities of language teachers, presented at the English Teaching Forum in April 1991.) The students perceived a good teacher as having the following qualities or doing the following things, in order from most to least important:

1. She believed in me, and made me believe in myself.
2. She made sure everyone understood.
3. We did the lesson together.
4. She let the students do it by themselves.
5. She used movements to make meaning clear.
6. She talked about the lesson.
7. She read in a tone that made meaning clear.
8. She talked about other subjects.
9. We did group work.
10. We played games.

The bad teacher was seen as one who exhibited these qualities:

1. She was very strict.
2. She shouted for no reason.
3. She didn't let us speak.
4. She was very nervous and bad tempered.
5. She didn't smile.
6. She forced us to do things.
7. She gave marks all the time.
8. She always spoke above our heads and dominated things.
9. She gave a lot of tests.
10. She started the lesson immediately.

1. What insights do the results of this survey offer you?

_____

_____

2. Which of the positive and negative actions or characteristics listed relate to your own? Of the positive ones, which you would like to enhance? Among the negative ones, which would you like to lessen?

Positive traits/actions: _____

Negative traits/actions: _____

3. How would the responses differ if the surveyed students had been adults?

_____

_____

4. If your students were given the same survey, what would their responses be?

_____

_____

5. Conduct the survey with your students. Are their responses as you predicted? What do the results tell you?

_____

_____

Task 2

1. From the list below, circle the five adjectives that best describe you as a teacher.

interesting	solid	loving
stimulating	reliable	neat
engaging	patient	modest
exciting	motivated	sensitive
enthusiastic	gentle	principled
imaginative	friendly	considerate
hardworking	cheerful	devoted
creative	firm	flexible
encouraging	consistent	precise
caring	decisive	sensible
warm	sympathetic	self-directed
outgoing	organized	innovative
emphatic	stubborn	rational
committed	pleasant	understanding

What does your selection tell you?

---

2. In *Teaching by Principles*, Brown describes a positive feature he terms "classroom energy." He explains that "through whatever role or style you accomplish this, you do so through solid preparation, confidence in your ability to teach, a genuinely positive belief in your students' ability to learn, a sense of joy in doing what you do, and you also do so by overtly manifesting that preparation, confidence, positive belief, and joy when you walk into the classroom" (p. 422). Which of the qualities Brown mentions are strong and weak points for you?

---

3. Characteristics and abilities such as warmth, empathy, genuineness, negotiating and listening skills, and positive attitudes are necessary for teachers. In an article posted in *The Language Teacher Online*, Adrian Underhill claims that "These personal and interpersonal factors are not fixed, that they can be brought to awareness, observed, talked about, reflected on, practised and improved significantly." In your teacher preparation courses, were these factors addressed? Do you agree with Underhill's statement that these factors can, in some sense, be taught and learned?

Task 3

While in the classroom, we are constantly observed by our students, who examine not only our work but every detail of our appearance. This makes some teachers (especially beginners) believe that appearance contributes to effectiveness.

1. Have you ever thought about this? How important do you think appearance is, compared to other factors?

_____

_____

2. Do you think your students have certain expectations related to your attire? What are they?

_____

_____

3. How do you feel on the first day with a new group of students, when they actually do seem to focus on the way you look, talk, and behave?

_____

_____

Teacher Motivation and Attitude

It is generally accepted that our attitude toward teaching has a significant influence in the classroom. It accounts to some degree not only for our own teaching successes and weaknesses, but can also affect students' learning. Attitudes seem to generate attitudes: the attitudes we have toward our assignments induce students' attitudes and behaviors.

In a 1989 article, Donald Freeman provides a comprehensive definition of *attitude*:

> Attitude is here defined as the stance one adopts toward oneself, the activity of teaching, and the learners one engages in the teaching/learning process. Attitude is an interplay of externally oriented behavior, actions, and perceptions, on the one hand, and internal intrapersonal dynamics, feelings, and reactions, on the other. It becomes a sort of bridge that influences the effective functioning of the individual teacher in particular circumstances. As such, it can begin to account for the differential successes, strengths, and weaknesses of individual teachers (p. 32).

Task 1

Reflect on your commitment and attitude.

1. Overall, how would you rate your commitment to your students?

        5   4   3   2   1
Highly committed   Could be more committed

2. Try to remember your former teachers. What were the qualities and attitudes of those you particularly liked and thought of as effective?

Personal: _____

Professional: _____

3. What were the qualities and attitudes of teachers you did not like and did not view as effective?

Personal: _____

Professional: _____

4. What conclusions can you draw?

_____

_____

Task 2

Classroom behaviors can be a direct result of teacher and student attitudes. Think about your own teaching style while you complete the questions in this task.

1. List some teacher behaviors to which students respond positively, and a few that they dislike or would not approve of.

Effective behavior	Ineffective behavior
well prepared for class	unprepared and improvises
keeps notes, teaching materials, and plans well organized	disorganized

2. What are some things your students praise you for? Do any of your actions give them cause to complain?

_____

_____

3. Do you think your students have clear ideas about how you should behave? If so, how would they define them?

_____

_____

4. How do students react when teachers do not meet their expectations?

_____

_____

5. You may have talked with your students about their responsibilities—perhaps even creating a list of them to post in the classroom—but have you ever created a list of your own responsibilities to share with your students?

Yes ❑   No ❑

6. How useful do you think such a list would be? If you do not have such a list, create one and post it in your classroom. Be sure your students are aware of it, and try to stand by the items you list. What do you observe?

_____

_____

Task 3

The word *enthusiastic* in the context of education evokes an image of a pleasant learning atmosphere, with teachers radiating energy and joy for everything they do. Enthusiasm guarantees teachers' profound commitment and attachment to their job and a positive way of dealing with stress. In general, it seems that teachers who have this positive characteristic outside the classroom bring it inside as well.

1. How enthusiastic are you about what you are doing?

       5   4   3   2   1
Very enthusiastic   Not enthusiastic

2. Are you happy with what you do?   Yes ❑   No ❑   I don't know ❑

3. Is there a positive and supportive link between your personal and professional lives?
Yes ❏   No ❏   I don't know ❏

4. How would you rate your overall attitude toward teaching?

    5   4   3   2   1
Positive   Negative

5. If possible, videotape yourself while teaching. How enthusiastic and motivated do you appear to be? Does the tape show something different from the response you gave to question 1?

_____

_____

6. As Julia Chemali put it in an article in *TESL Contact*, "The teacher who combines knowledge with excitement is the one who can hold the student's attention." Do you agree? How does this relate to your own qualities as a teacher?

_____

_____

Task 4

Certain teacher qualities seem to be prerequisite for achieving peak performance within certain teaching settings.

1. In your opinion, what are the most important qualities for any teacher? And what are the most important qualities for teachers of learners of various ages?

Qualities important in any setting	Qualities important for teaching adults	Qualities important for teaching high school students	Qualities important for teaching middle/junior high school students	Qualities important for teaching elementary students
_____	_____	_____	_____	_____
_____	_____	_____	_____	_____
_____	_____	_____	_____	_____
_____	_____	_____	_____	_____
_____	_____	_____	_____	_____

2. How has the fact that you teach a certain age group influenced your life, your professional development, and your career in general? Which of your qualities has it enhanced?

_____

_____

3. Do you enjoy teaching the age group you teach? What are the positives and negatives?

_____

_____

Your Overall Well-Being

Be grateful when you're feeling good and graceful when you're feeling bad.
RICHARD CARLSON, *DON'T SWEAT THE SMALL STUFF...
AND IT'S ALL SMALL STUFF*

Most (or maybe all?) teachers work in highly stressful environments. Common complaints focus on the enormous workload, problems with student behavior, anxiety over not knowing what the future holds, and difficulty coping with extra responsibilities added to daily schedules. Considering the magnitude of the problem and the fact that working conditions rarely change, it is essential that teachers be provided with support to cope with the existing situation. Unfortunately, in most contexts there is not enough done to help teachers ease the stress. Instead, teachers have to develop their own coping strategies, with possibilities including the following:

- adapting to a higher level of tolerance;
- avoiding stressful situations completely or whenever possible;
- asking for a transfer;
- resigning or taking early retirement;
- changing professions; or
- developing techniques to cope with stress (exercise, meditation, etc.).

You will probably agree that the last option is by far the most constructive, but at the same time it may be the most difficult to implement.

Task 1

1. Many would agree that stress is caused not only by circumstances themselves but by the way we react to them. How do you react to stress and cope with it? Are you satisfied with the results of your approach?

Stressful situation	How do you feel?	How do you usually react?	Does your reaction help alleviate the stress?
_____	_____	_____	_____
_____	_____	_____	_____
_____	_____	_____	_____
_____	_____	_____	_____
_____	_____	_____	_____

2. If you work in a highly stressful setting and as a consequence are not enthusiastic about what you do, can you identify the factors that contribute to this situation? Indicate the degree of stress caused by each factor.

Factor	Result
_____	_____
_____	_____
_____	_____
_____	_____
_____	_____

3. Which of the preceding factors are within your power to change?

_____

_____

4. There are numerous books on coping with stress. What techniques do they usually offer? Would they work for you?

_____

_____

5. Many people affirm the "power of positive thinking." As Henry Ford said, "Whether you think you can or you think you can't, you are right." A high school teacher we know created a positive statement —"I am confident that I can be fully in charge of my current group of students"—and repeated it to herself daily with what she claimed were very positive results. Create your own statement, and try out this method to see if it works for you. What are your observations?

Statement: _____

_____

_____

6. Another way of easing stress is by helping others. Think about your past teaching week. Did you do anything that made a difference for anyone? Are you planning to help any of your colleagues with anything they find challenging?

_____

_____

Task 2

Allotting some time for your favorite leisure activities and giving yourself the opportunity to "recharge" is equally important as allotting time, effort, and attention to your family, friends, students, and professional assignments.

1. How do you usually feel before and after each class and at the end of the day?

_____

_____

2. Do you give yourself periods of peace and quiet during your teaching day?

_____

_____

3. Do you feel that you don't have enough time for yourself? Is your life "all work and no play"? If so, monitor your daily schedule for about a week, noting time spent on activities not related to your work or on necessary domestic tasks. Is there a good balance between your work and leisure activities?

Day	Leisure activity	Workload
Monday		
Tuesday		
Wednesday		
Thursday		
Friday		
Saturday		
Sunday		

212

4. What can you conclude from the preceding chart?

_____

_____

Task 3

At the end of their first year, teachers usually fall into one of two categories: they either feel good about themselves and admire their knowledge (and are sometimes unaware of how much there is still to be learned!) or they feel gloomy about their work and believe they may not be suited to the job. Like everyone, teachers can be very harsh critics of themselves. Indeed, in *A Course in Language Teaching*, Penny Ur, one of the most widely admired figures in ESL teaching today, mentions experiencing just such feelings at the beginning of her career.

How did you feel about your qualities and accomplishments as a teacher at the end of your first year? How do you feel about them today?

_____

_____

Teacher-Student Relationships

The teacher-student relationship is not uncommonly a special one, and one that may resonate throughout a lifetime. Students often recognize former teachers as "theirs," even after many years have passed, and award them a special place in their memories.

Students of all ages respond positively to teachers who show interest in and respect for them as individuals, and who provide all the support they need. This attitude in the classroom creates not only a positive learning environment but a positive life experience.

Task 1

1. Analyze the relationship you develop with your students. Video- or audiotapes of your teaching may help as you complete this task.

	Always 5	4	3	2	Not at all 1
Awareness of students:					
I know the names of all my students.					
I know the family situations of all my students.					
I inquire about students' personal accomplishments and interests.					
I know which of my students are visual, tactile, or auditory learners.					
My students with visual or aural impairments are seated close to the chalkboard or to the position from which I most often teach.					
I dress according to my students' expectations.					
Classroom interaction:					
I always greet my students and acknowledge their presence.					
I always smile when greeting them.					
I try to create a friendly, supportive, and nonthreatening atmosphere.					
I tell and listen to jokes and stories.					
I often point out the humorous side of a situation.					
I try to make my students laugh as often as I can.					
I have a compassionate, warm, but firm attitude toward students.					
I use small talk before and after class.					
I try to make each of my students feel important.					
I use gestures and body language to enliven the class.					
I display enthusiasm and humor.					
I project confidence, strength, and optimism.					
Support:					
I am willing to help students during breaks, but I make them aware that I need some rest time, too.					
I am an active listener and try to see the other person's point of view, using the information gained to respond effectively.					

	Always				Not at all
	5	4	3	2	1
I show sensitivity to students' developmental levels and cultural backgrounds.					
I help students organize their new knowledge.					
I let students operate equipment and distribute materials.					
I help students develop strategies for learning and communication.					
In general, I am willing to go out of my way for others.					

2. What are your particular strengths and weaknesses, as revealed by the preceding chart? What can you do to correct the weaknesses?

_____

_____

Task 2

Conduct an experiment: dedicate one of your teaching days to studying your students' emotions, both while you teach and as they do classroom activities.

1. Are your students worried, anxious, happy, unhappy, frustrated, joyful, relaxed or...? Look at their faces. Are they smiling, laughing, frowning?

_____

_____

2. What do their emotions tell you?

_____

_____

3. Do you see any signs of personal problems among the students? If so, what do you view as your role in this situation?

_____

_____

4. Can these observations help you in any way? How? Is there anything you need to do?

_____

_____

215

Task 3

In many cultures, teachers are perceived as authorities and are addressed with the highest possible level of respect. If you teach adults who have been exposed to such educational systems, this fact needs to be taken into consideration. For example, many may be uncomfortable being addressed by their first name and may not want to address those in "authority" in this way.

1. How do your students address you? How do you address them? How do they address each other? Do you sense any discomfort on their part over this issue?

_____

_____

2. How do you address your colleagues and supervisors? How do they address you?

_____

_____

3. To what extent do forms of address matter in your teaching context?

_____

_____

Task 4

Think about the way you react to events in your classroom.

1. Try to recall an incident when your students pleasantly surprised you. What did they do? What was your reaction?

_____

_____

2. Recall an incident when your students did something you found irritating. How did you react? Did you make them aware of the problem? How?

_____

_____

3. Would you react the same way again? Why?

_____

_____

14. Assessment, Testing, and Marking

The terms *assessment*, *evaluation*, and *testing* have considerably different connotations across the literature, though *assessment* and *evaluation* are quite often used interchangeably. In this book, we reserve *evaluation* to refer only to program evaluation; *assessment* is used to indicate a collection of techniques and methods intended to determine students' proficiency, progress, or achievement, and to diagnose weak areas.

Within the broad scope of assessment there are two generally recognized categories: quantitative and qualitative. The former includes procedures based on formal tests conducted with a variety of objectives in mind, along with other data-gathering techniques such as attendance records, ratings, and questionnaires. Qualitative assessment includes such things as classroom observation, interviews, case studies, student portfolios, student self-assessment, group projects, and student presentations.

This chapter provides opportunities for you to re-examine your testing methods, marking, and overall assessment of students, and offers ideas on how to encourage students to self-assess.

Testing

> *Know then thyself, presume not God to scan,*
> *The proper study of mankind is man.*
> ALEXANDER POPE, *AN ESSAY ON MAN*

Most students (and many teachers) have quite ambivalent feelings about tests. They dread or claim to hate them, but at the same time they demonstrate curiosity about results, waiting anxiously to see their marks or asking repeatedly when the results will be tabulated.

Tests seem to be a necessary tool, used for a variety of purposes: to determine proficiency levels to guide initial student placement, to measure progress throughout a course, to identify particular problem areas where students may need extra help, and, at the end of a term or course, to determine how well students have met objectives. Such tests are often referred to as "formal."

Task 1

Placement tests are used to determine students' general proficiency at the beginning of a program for the purposes of placing them in appropriate groups and tailoring instruction to a particular proficiency level. They are often administered in adult education settings, noncredit courses, and language-learning programs.

1. If you teach in one of these contexts, how are students directed to your class? Do you have any role in determining who will be in your class? If students are not tested centrally, how do you assess general proficiency to determine which instructional techniques, materials, and procedures you should use?

_____

_____

2. In many programs, a formal placement test is used in conjunction with informal assessment to guide decisions about grouping for instruction. On the basis of an initial placement test, students are divided into different classes; then, during the first few classes, teachers have a chance to reassess proficiency levels based on classroom interaction and participation and can recommend movement of particular students.

How do you reassess students during the first few classes? How do you use the results of that assessment?

_____

_____

Task 2

Some tests are administered during a course to determine students' progress. They may also be used for diagnostic purposes to point out to students and the teacher areas that need attention. Achievement tests are administered at the end of a course to determine how students have met program objectives.

1. Consider the methods and techniques of testing that you use in order to determine student progress or how well the students have met program objectives. What skills and areas do you test?

_____

_____

2. How do the skills and areas you test correspond to what you teach?

_____

_____

3. Do you test certain subskills within each of the skills (e.g., scanning and skimming within the area of reading)?

_____

_____

218

4. What testing techniques do you use? Circle those that you rely on most heavily.

essay questions	unscrambling
short-answer questions	cloze
multiple-choice questions	finding synonyms and antonyms
true-false statements	interviews
free writing	role-plays
guided writing	story retelling
sentence construction	audio- or videotaping
paraphrasing	student presentations
summarizing	problem solving
sentence combining	completion of specific tasks
sentence completion	other:
fill in the blanks	

Additional Possibilities for Language Teachers:

transformations	minimal pair discrimination
translation	intonation pattern discrimination
discrimination	reading aloud
reading blanked dialogue	dictogloss
describing pictures	dictation
describing picture stories	other:

5. Discuss the methods you use with your colleagues. Do they use any techniques that you do not? If so, try them out and take notes on how they work.

_____

_____

6. Are your tests designed primarily to indicate what students have already learned or to diagnose what they still need to learn?

_____

_____

Task 3

The best tests not only give us information about our students and programs, but they also serve as effective learning tools.

1. To ensure that students find your tests useful, do you ask them for feedback? Why or why not? If you do, what procedures do you use?

_____

_____

2. How do you ensure that students benefit as much as possible from the tests you give them?

	Always				Never
	5	4	3	2	1
I design tests so that the majority of students will be reasonably successful at them.					
I take up the tests in class.					
When I mark tests I indicate correct answers so that students can see where they went wrong.					
I mark tests clearly and provide positive feedback.					
I have students self-correct tests or exchange tests with a friend for marking.					
I apologize when a test has been too difficult.					
I follow up with extra practice where necessary.					
I mark tests promptly so students still remember what each one was about and are motivated to learn the correct responses.					

3. Is there anything in your testing practice that needs improvement or that you would like to alter?

Yes ❏   No ❏   I don't know ❏

4. Even in noncredit courses, it can still be meaningful to test at regular intervals to check what students have grasped. Tests can cover material taught during a defined time period, and as a follow-up, students can work in groups to discuss their answers and provide a rationale for them. This usually generates a great deal of discussion, during which students explain how they feel about their responses. Correct answers are then taken up with the whole class.

Have you ever tried this strategy? If so, what were the results? If not, do you think it could be useful?

_____

_____

5. Another productive strategy for making tests a learning experience rather than a stressful one is to ask students, after correct answers have been taken up, to write down items they feel still need more work. Collecting responses and analyzing them provides valuable insight into what

needs to be reviewed before teaching new items. Have you ever tried this strategy for gaining student feedback?

_____

_____

6. Students often complain about "surprise" tests, tests that include items that they did not expect, and tests that take unanticipated formats. How do you prepare students for tests without revealing too much information? Do you feel that some element of surprise is useful? If so, to what extent?

_____

_____

Task 4

Analyze the last test you administered and answer the following questions to help you determine your testing strengths and weaknesses.

1. Did you test what you taught?   Yes ❑   No ❑

2. Were the instructions short and clear?   Yes ❑   No ❑

3. Were the students familiar with the test format?   Yes ❑   No ❑

4. Were the students given an appropriate length of time to do the test?   Yes ❑   No ❑

5. Things I did effectively:

_____

_____

Things I did not do effectively:

_____

_____

6. Repeat this process two or three times until you have analyzed several recently administered tests. Are their weaknesses and strengths the same? Is there a pattern? What can you do to make your tests better?

_____

_____

Task 5

If you repeatedly teach the same course and reuse your tests, it may be a good idea to reflect on their effectiveness and completeness from time to time (and to make sure that copies are not circulating between your former and current students!). Next time you teach the course, complete the following chart to identify what you are teaching and what needs to be taught. Then, compare the completed chart to your old tests. Is there anything that needs to be changed, added, or deleted?

Unit/Topic taught	What needs to be tested?	Test question

Task 6

1. A test that actually measures what it is supposed to measure is said to be "valid." For example, a test of listening skills that consists of a very long recorded speech or conversation followed by twenty comprehension questions may not be valid since it may reveal more about students' memories than their ability to understand oral language. A test in a practical computer course that asks students to describe how to create tables in a word-processing program does little to indicate whether those students can effectively use that tool.

Analyze your last two tests and try to determine their validity.

What was the test intended to measure?	What did the test actually measure?

2. Another concept commonly mentioned in the literature about assessment is test "reliability." A test is not reliable if there are significant differences in the marks awarded by different evaluators. If you have a colleague with whom you feel comfortable and who teaches the same content as you do to students of similar age and proficiency, conduct an experiment. Before you mark your next test, each of you photocopy the work of four or five of your students and provide the other with a copy of those papers. Both of you should then mark your own tests and the ones se-

lected from your colleague's class, and then compare how the other evaluated the work. How do the corrections differ? What are the similarities? What conclusions can you draw? Which test-correction techniques that you currently use work well across tests? Which ones could be improved?

_____

_____

Marking

To determine how students are progressing, most teachers use an established system of assessment that involves assigning marks or grades on both quantitative and qualitative measures. It is no wonder that marking is one of the most common topics of conversation among students and teachers. What do teachers and students have to say about it? Both groups complain most of the time.

We compiled a list of common complaints and sources of frustration related to marking that are frequently heard among teachers and high school students:

Teachers' complaints	Students' complaints
"Students expect high marks even when they don't hand in half of their assignments or do not participate in class."	"Many teachers don't have a carefully thought-out marking scheme, so they're not clear on what elements they are marking in an assignment or on a test. In other words, they should decide what elements are worth how many marks before they start marking."
"It annoys me when top students complain about every half mark."	"Favoritism hurts. Teachers should mark the tests without looking at the names."
"Marking is such a time-consuming process that involves full concentration, and when I have time for it at the end of the day, it just drains me."	"Marking is always one-sided and subjective. Teachers don't care what you think you deserve. Many of them don't even bother to explain why you got the mark."
"Students are sometimes completely unrealistic—they ask for a mark they do not deserve."	"In order to get a good mark, you always have to do or write what the teacher wants, and adjust your style to the teacher's. We never get to do or write what we feel is important."
"What irritates me most is when parents come in to fight for marks. They don't have a clear picture of who is in class, and they don't know how many other students do a considerably better job than their son or daughter."	"Marking is always unfair to someone in class—usually to the students whose tests are corrected when the teacher is already fed up or simply does not have enough time or energy for them."
"Students often bother me for extensions on deadlines, and then they still expect to get high marks despite the fact that they are handing the assignment in late."	"Even if you complain, you still have to accept the mark the teacher assigns."

Teachers' complaints	Students' complaints
"I have a feeling that I waste too much energy on marking. It's simply not worth it."	"Teachers don't mark things quickly enough."
"I am too exhausted to create complicated marking schemes. Based on my experience, I can give a mark without resorting to math."	"Many teachers are very inconsistent. Even if they make their expectations clear, they don't adhere to them."
"It would be ideal to create common criteria for marking every test and use percentages for each of the elements that needs to be marked, but I simply do not have the energy to do that."	"I don't know what my current mark is and what I can expect at the end of the term. The teacher never tells me."
"I have no life because of marking. I loathe it with passion."	

Task 1

1. Many marking-related problems can be avoided. Create a list of tips for teachers based on your experience and the degree to which you think the preceding complaints—both teachers' and students'—are legitimate.

Marking do's	Marking don'ts

2. How content are you with your current marking methods? Do you feel that anything needs to be changed? Are there any obstacles to changing your current approach?

_____

_____

Teaching for the Test

In some programs, there is considerable emphasis on students' taking and passing a proficiency or standardized test that will determine whether they will be able to pursue particular educational or career goals. Examples include the Test of English as a Foreign Language (TOEFL) or Test of English for International Communication (TOEIC) for language learners, or the Scholastic Aptitude Test

(SAT) required for admission to most universities in the United States. Needless to say, students in such programs are under an enormously magnified pressure to succeed, often in a short time span.

Today, many proficiency tests used for admission purposes by academic institutions and professional associations include components that assess a range of skills. Not so long ago, however, it was possible for students to score well on a test but not be able to apply their knowledge. In our experience in ESL programs, for example, it was not uncommon for students to excel on a proficiency test focusing on receptive skills of grammar, reading, and listening but to be quite unable to carry on an everyday conversation or write a meaningful paragraph. Frustrated teachers who tried to "teach the students some English" while preparing them for the test had to use various tricks of the trade to divert students' attention from books of sample test questions and engage in an interactive activity or use authentic material.

1. If you teach a class with a strong focus on preparing students for a test, what is your approach? Place a checkmark in the appropriate column to indicate your strengths and any areas that may require some attention.

	Strong point	Needs improvement
My program covers all the skills and areas that appear on the test.		
I allot a proper amount of time to each skill and area, based on students' needs.		
After conducting practice tests I help students diagnose problem areas.		
I teach test-taking skills: predicting, inferring, guessing, reading or listening between the lines, skimming, scanning, etc.		
I teach how to understand the gist without necessarily knowing all the vocabulary, phrases, and references.		
I teach how to use morphological clues such as roots, prefixes, and suffixes to guess the meaning of unknown key words.		
I encourage students to monitor their progress by recording their results for each skill after each practice test.		
I add authentic reading and listening material to the course resources.		

2. If you indicated that any of these areas need work, what is your action plan for improvement?

_____

_____

_____

_____

Qualitative Assessment

Tests are not the only tool teachers can use to assess students' proficiency level, monitor progress, and determine the results of their teaching. Techniques of qualitative assessment, often referred to as "informal testing" (despite the fact that this name downplays their considerable value), are gaining more and more ground as sources of vital information that cannot be obtained by quantitative measures.

Task 1

1. Which of the following techniques of qualitative assessment do you use?

classroom observations   student self-assessment

interviews   group projects

case studies   student presentations

student portfolios   Other: _____

2. How do you monitor your students' participation in class activities and your students' progress?

_____

_____

3. How do you keep track of your observations?

_____

_____

4. Compare your students' results on tests with the information you gain through qualitative techniques. What do you glean from the comparison?

_____

_____

5. Do you keep students aware of the results of all your assessments?

_____

_____

Student Self-Assessment

Change is not made without inconvenience, even from worse to better.
SAMUEL JOHNSON, *A DICTIONARY OF THE ENGLISH LANGUAGE*

Self-assessment encourages students to take responsibility for their own learning and to monitor their own progress.

Task 1

1. Place a checkmark next to the techniques you use or encourage your students to use to promote self-evaluation.

— Learning journals
— Self- and peer marking of tests
— Peer correction of written work
— Questionnaires about their performance related to various aspects of the program
— Self-evaluation forms and grids
— Action plans to help students keep track of course objectives as they are completed
— A file of students' work for their perusal and evaluation
— Portfolios
— Peer evaluation of student presentations or projects
— Other: _____

2. Ask your students to assess themselves according to the points listed below. (You can add more statements to the list or adjust it to your group of students.)

	True	Somewhat true	Not true
I was present in class every day.			
I was always on time.			
I was always in class on time after break.			
I stayed in class from the beginning of the lesson to the end.			
I participated in all class activities.			
I participated in all field trips.			
I took notes in class.			
I asked questions.			

	True	Somewhat true	Not true
I kept my handouts and materials organized.			
I did work at home.			
I tried to use what I learned in class in the "real world."			
I made friends in class.			
I respected my classmates.			
I respected the teacher.			
Other: _____			

3. Find out how your students feel about this kind of self-assessment. How useful do they find it?

_____

_____

4. How can the results of this survey improve your program?

_____

_____

15. Program Evaluation

In the past few decades, program evaluation has received increasing attention as integral to the teaching process. Although there are a multitude of definitions and interpretations of the word *evaluation*, there seems to be general agreement about its overall value. In *The Elements of Language Curriculum*, for example, James Dean Brown describes it as "the glue that connects and holds together" all the elements of curriculum development and program delivery: needs analysis, objectives, materials, teaching, and testing.

In this chapter, we use Nunan and Lamb's understanding of evaluation, as enunciated in *The Self-Directed Teacher*:

> Evaluation involves the collection of information for the purposes of deciding what works and what does not work. This information is used to decide what aspects of an educational program should be left alone and what should be changed. A good evaluation will also offer advice on how changes might be brought about (p. 231).

Like Nunan and Lamb, in this book we also distinguish *evaluation* from *assessment*, a term reserved for descriptions of what students can or cannot do.

A review of the professional literature in this area reveals different approaches to program evaluation and numerous dimensions that shape points of view about it. The types of evaluation most commonly mentioned include the following:

- formative—conducted during the program with the purpose of bringing improvement;
- summative—conducted at the conclusion of the program to determine its effectiveness;
- process—focused on how the program works;
- product—focused on whether program goals have been achieved;
- quantitative—including countable bits of information (test results, statistical data);
- qualitative—including more holistic information based on observation, journal entries, etc.;
- outside—conducted by someone other than the teacher (students, peers, supervisors, or complete outsiders to the program, such as the representatives of funding or accreditation institutions); and
- inside—self-evaluation of teachers by teachers, or of students by students.

Outside and inside evaluation are often equated, respectively, with formal evaluation (conducted by others, especially supervisors) and informal evaluation (conducted by teachers themselves). Today, however, action research is facilitating the formalization of self-evaluation, which is included increasingly as a component of overall evaluation, so there may no longer be a clear distinction between the two. The same applies to other forms of program evaluation: summative evaluation becomes formative when it is used to revise and improve the next "run" of the program; quantitative information may be analyzed from a qualitative perspective.

Program evaluation, then, can be seen as quite broad and inclusive. It may include evaluation of many aspects of the program, may be conducted by different parties both from inside and outside, and may utilize a variety of instruments and procedures. Since the focus of this book is teacher self-evaluation, this chapter concentrates on course and teacher evaluation as done by students, by teachers, and by supervisors.

The Truth May Hurt (But It Helps Us Learn)

The ego has always been a paradox—it is the point from which you see, but it also makes you blind.
BILL RUSSELL, *SECOND WIND*

It would be helpful if someone could provide us with ten easy steps to taming our egos but, failing that, we must develop our own strategies and techniques for doing so. This is difficult to accomplish because, quite simply, criticism hurts. But if we do not prepare ourselves mentally to receive constructive criticism with a view to changing our patterns, then conducting program evaluation will be a waste of time.

Once a teacher does decide to undertake such an evaluation, there are a number of things that must be kept in mind:

- Program evaluation takes courage. Don't do it until you are absolutely ready, or it will only result in frustration for both you and your students.
- Prepare yourself to face both positive and negative comments. The positive ones may boost your self-esteem, but it is the negative comments that shed a different light on your perception of your teaching and facilitate the self-improvement process.
- Only constructive criticism helps, so make sure whoever is conducting the evaluation knows what that means.
- Many teachers believe that program evaluation often results in loss of face. The truth is that, regardless of the results, your willingness to undertake such an evaluation demonstrates only your very positive desire to improve. This is not a test; there are no wrong answers or bad marks, but just opinions about your teaching viewed from different perspectives.
- In some cultures it is considered completely inappropriate for students to evaluate their teachers. If your class includes students from such cultures and your program evaluation will include solicitation of student responses, extra preparation will need to be undertaken to explain the benefits of the evaluation.

Although it is clear that program evaluation is beneficial, a great deal of research remains to be done to determine the extent of its value. Since you are holding this book in your hands and are reading this chapter, you are obviously interested in exploring this area. You may be a pioneer whose willingness to undertake program evaluation will help us all understand how and why it can contribute to improved teaching practice.

Task 1

A high school teacher asked her students to evaluate her course at the end of the year. Students obviously had a bone to pick with her, and welcomed what they saw as an opportunity to point out her weaknesses. Most of their evaluation sheets revealed the same deficiency: during her lessons, she would immerse herself totally with the weaker students and, as a result, other students' needs were overlooked; furthermore, because the same tasks were assigned to everyone in the class, stronger students often ended up twiddling their thumbs or reading magazines toward the end of lessons. When the teacher read the evaluation sheets, she was terribly upset. She announced that she would never conduct an evaluation in her class again. She commented further that she generally had no problems with criticism, as long as it was not direct criticism of her performance.

What do you think the teacher was trying to accomplish with the survey? What do you think about her level of preparation for it? What does this vignette tell you about the culture of high school students?

_____

_____

_____

_____

Task 2

In *The Elements of Language Curriculum*, Brown states that conducting regular evaluation puts staff in a better position to "defend" the program against external pressures. What benefits of conducting program evaluation do you see in your teaching context?

_____

_____

Evaluation by Students

When things are done the same old way, the same old results can be expected.
JOHNNETTA B. COLE, *DREAM THE BOLDEST DREAMS*

No one can provide better feedback on overall course quality than students. This may seem obvious but, in practice, it is often overlooked. We tend to forget that students can be the best teacher trainers. Their insights and perceptions regarding our lessons, performance, and professionalism can assist us in building clearer and more objective images of the quality of our teaching and in identifying areas that need to be improved.

Task 1

Teachers who ask their students for feedback should be prepared for a range of responses—from open, constructive comments on evaluation surveys to negative reactions or signs of disapproval on students' faces during lessons.

1. Do you remember any student comments—either positive or negative—that have had a profound effect on you, personally or professionally?

_____

_____

2. Try to recall a negative comment. What was it related to?

_____

_____

3. Analyze the action that triggered the negative reaction or comment. Was there anything you could have done differently? Was there anything your students should have done differently?

_____

_____

Task 2

In my continuous-intake TOEFL class, I [Hanna] conducted regular program evaluation by means of soliciting students' responses. Two issues became evident in the course of these evaluations:

- Students from some cultures were very comfortable with program evaluation and offered constructive criticism right from the outset, while students from other cultures needed time to get used to the idea of participating in the process.
- Students who were initially uncomfortable gained a better understanding of the process and offered more detailed feedback after I explained the purpose and importance of the evaluation and after they participated in several evaluation activities.

Do these issues relate to your teaching context? How do you address them? Might a different approach have a positive effect?

_____

_____

Task 3

Program evaluation is most often conducted at the end of a course, when students are asked to list positive points, identify problem areas, and suggest changes with the benefit of a clear image of what has been taught, how, and with what results. It seems to us equally valid, however, to obtain student feedback as a course gets under way. If you were standing at an intersection and were not entirely sure of which road to take, how would you decide which way to go? You might stop a passerby and ask for directions. At the end of the first teaching week of a course or semester, you may be standing at such an intersection, and your students are the passersby who can confirm which route to take in terms of course content, instructional method, classroom atmosphere, and resources and learning materials. They have been exposed to enough of your teaching style and methodology, and by this time you will have explained the course content, so they will be able to tell you whether they feel that something needs to be altered to maximize their learning. Their responses are useful for diagnostic purposes and can be the most valuable predictor of how your class will unfold. They may be the eye-opener that prompts you to reorganize the course or to make minor cosmetic changes.

1. Create a list of questions for your students that you might use as an end-of-the-first-week program evaluation.

_____

_____

_____

_____

2. After the first week of your next course or semester, pose the questions. What are the results? How do the results affect your thinking about how the course will proceed?

_____

_____

3. Try conducting a similar survey informally and orally, perhaps every week or few days. Ask questions such as "How do you feel about this? How much more practice do you need? What do you think about this type of activity?" If you are a novice teacher, you could add, "I've never tried this activity before, and I'd like to know how you feel about it." Does this sort of informal evaluation have an impact on your program and practice? Does expressing this sort of interest in your students' learning preferences affect the classroom atmosphere?

_____

_____

Task 4

Conducting a student survey at the end of a unit may provide ideas for improvement for the next time you teach the same content. An "end of the unit" evaluation questionnaire might ask students to rate the unit's usefulness and importance, the degree of difficulty of its various components, the elements they found most and least enjoyable, how well its purposes were realized, and how motivated they were by it, and ask for students' suggestions for improvement.

Design such a questionnaire to solicit student evaluation of your next unit. What are the results? Why is undertaking such an evaluation useful? How do the students view it?

_____

_____

_____

_____

Supervisory Evaluation

A heated debate on the benefits of supervisors observing in classrooms took place in August 1998 on the TESL-L electronic bulletin board operated out of the City University of New York. Complaints about the practice included its anxiety-producing aspects and the fact that it was in many cases a waste of time, since teachers "put on a show" and "follow the party line" when a supervisor is in the room. Most of the proponents of supervisory observation acknowledged the potential danger of basing decisions on promotions and rehiring on it, but at the same time expressed the belief that observation facilitates the reflective process of professional development and should be conducted with that purpose in mind.

Bruce Rindler of Boston University posted a message on the bulletin board in which he described a study he had undertaken. More than 400 full-time faculty in intensive English programs across the United States were asked to complete a questionnaire and respond to open-ended questions on such aspects of evaluation as the techniques used, the person who conducts the evaluation, the environment, feedback provided, and the attributes of the teacher being evaluated. Two main factors emerged as those determining the value of classroom observations for the teacher being observed: the nature of the feedback and the evaluator. Feedback that was detailed, informed, and insightful was appreciated and received more positively; the more credible, trusted, and knowledgeable the evaluator, the more persuasive and useful the observed teacher felt the feedback to be.

Sian Baldwin of Beirut shared suggestions put forward by teachers at her institution. The staff had unanimously requested that they be judged primarily on observations, as they felt that this method was the best measure of teacher performance. They asked that they be observed by the same person at least four times during the year. Also, they wanted to be given the opportunity of requesting another observer, in the event they felt uncomfortable with the one who had been chosen. Other discussion participants suggested that the observer also be a teacher (preferably a practicing one with considerable experience), that the observations be preceded by a short discussion and followed by a longer one, and that they be multiple rather than sporadic, as this increases the observed teacher's opportunities to demonstrate effective teaching.

Task 1

1. What is your opinion on supervisory evaluation? What do you see as its benefits and disadvantages?

_____

_____

2. If you feel that the model of supervisory evaluation now in place in your school or department is not effective, how do you think it ought to be changed?

_____

_____

Task 2

At the beginning of my career, I [Vesna] taught at a high school. One day an evaluator came in and sat right next to the weakest student in the room, someone who skipped most classes and whose binder was half empty. This was a bad sign, and I sensed that things would not be going all that smoothly for my evaluation. Things did indeed go from bad to worse. The equipment, around which the whole lesson was built, broke down right in the middle of things. An extra bulb for the overhead projector was nowhere to be found, and neither was a colleague who usually helped me out with technical problems. The rest of the lesson felt like a struggle for survival, and I prayed throughout that Murphy's law wouldn't take its full toll. But ever since, I have always made sure to have a spare bulb in my pocket and a back-up cassette player ready before presentations or classes begin—just in case.

Murphy's law for teachers might read, "Anything that can go wrong during a lesson, will go wrong while your supervisor is in the room." Many teachers have funny stories (at least in retrospect) to tell about supervisory evaluation. Has anything similar to my experience happened in your class?

_____

_____

Task 3

A teacher's wish list regarding desirable qualities for a supervisor might include the following:

- the ability to motivate teachers and help them work to their full potential;
- good listening and people skills;
- professionalism;
- expertise and experience; and
- approachability and availability.

1. What additional things would you add to this list? Why?

_____

_____

_____

2. At some point in all of our careers, we have been evaluated formally. How do you feel about your evaluation experiences?

_____

_____

3. Do you have a chance to offer feedback, explanations, or clarifications?

_____

_____

4. Is there anything you would like to change about the way supervisory observations are conducted in your teaching context?

_____

_____

Task 4

Both of us have had the opportunity in our careers to gain years of classroom teaching practice and to observe numerous adult ESL classes in a variety of programs. Based on our experience, we feel that supervision should be guided by these two underlying principles:

- observing effective and ineffective teacher behaviors, learning from them, and then helping others acquire that knowledge; and
- encouraging teachers to self-evaluate and learn from the process.

1. How much of their knowledge do your supervisors share with you? How useful do you find it?

_____

_____

2. Have your supervisors encouraged you to self-evaluate?   Yes ❑   No ❑

3. How does "delivered wisdom" from supervisors compare to what you have learned on your own, through the process of self-evaluation?

_____

_____

16. Professional Development

The time when one graduated from high school, college, or university equipped with all the skills and knowledge necessary for the next thirty or forty years of professional practice is long gone. With new theories and methods continually being developed, questioned, and re-examined, and with science and technology changing at a rapid rate, the need for career-long learning is a reality we all have to accept.

Research or Practice?

Do teachers learn more from their own classroom experience and their "on the spot" experiments and action research than they do from published results of research studies? Is teaching a profession or a trade? A possible answer to these questions is offered by Carr and Kemmis, quoted in a 1987 *TESOL Quarterly* article by Jack Richards:

> One indication of the degree of professionalization of a field is the extent to which the methods and procedures employed by members of a profession are based on a body of theoretical knowledge and research.

Task 1

1. Obviously, in our first few years in the classroom, we base our practice on the knowledge gained in teacher preparation courses. Place a checkmark next to the areas of study that were included in your own preservice program.

— discipline-specific knowledge
— classroom-based research
— critical pedagogy
— cross-cultural communication
— curriculum and syllabus design
— assessment
— methodology
— technology in the classroom
— Other: _____

2. If there are any areas that were not covered in your teacher preparation program, how did you go about gaining knowledge in them? If there are areas with which you are unfamiliar, how could you go about exploring them?

_____

_____

_____

_____

Task 2

As a student and probably at some point in your teaching career, you have had a chance to observe other teachers at work. Some of them may have been excellent, but it is likely that others did not impress you.

1. Skill in teaching derives from a combination of discipline-specific knowledge and an understanding of pedagogy and methodology, interpersonal skills, and personal qualities. What are the attributes that distinguish a good teacher from a mediocre one, or a truly inspiring teacher from a good one? What are the characteristics of effective teachers?

	Very important			Less important	
Attributes	5	4	3	2	1
Inquisitiveness					
Tolerance					
Love of teaching					
Love of the subject matter					
People skills					
Creativity					
Empathy					
Dedication to ongoing professional development					
Willingness to do more and better					
Solid teacher training					
Positive attitude					
Flexibility					
Knowledge of methodology					
Knowledge of the subject matter					

2. What are your own strengths? What might you be able to do about any weaknesses?

_____

_____

_____

_____

Professional Development Options

A Socrates in every classroom....
A. WHITNEY GRISWOLD, *TIME*, 11 JUNE 1951

We have a responsibility to pursue ongoing professional development not only to improve our practice but also the image of our profession. The professional development options that might result in such an improved image include the following:

- networking through committees, conferences, and workshops;
- membership in professional associations;
- taking courses;
- disseminating good ideas by presenting at workshops, writing articles, and sharing materials; and
- staying informed about issues pertaining to the profession and field.

Task 1

1. Which of these options have you used recently?

_____

_____

2. Professional development is conducted in a multitude of ways. Study the list below and make notes about what you have done or plan to do in future.

Option	Details
Taking courses	
Exploring published research	
Reading professional publications	
Searching computer databases (e.g., ERIC) or the Internet for information on particular topics	

Option	Details
Attending workshops and conferences	
Participating in "swap shops" to exchange teaching materials and ideas	
Participating in inservice activities within your department or program	
Reviewing textbooks	
Developing new activities	
Sharing ideas and materials with colleagues	
Visiting resource centers and professional libraries	
Conducting self-evaluation or classroom research through	
action research	
peer observation	
checklists	
video- or audiorecording your teaching	
filling out your own observation report during supervisory evaluation	
portfolio assessment	
setting professional development goals and reflecting on the results	
Other:	

3. In our experience, teacher self-evaluation undertaken simultaneously by staff throughout a school, program, or department is very worthwhile. Participation should be voluntary, but we have found that teachers are often happy to participate if they know that their colleagues will be involved. By using tasks such as those described in this book, self-evaluation can become peer evaluation, and insights can be shared among colleagues.

Do you think such a project would be feasible in your teaching context? How valuable do you feel it would be? How could it be initiated?

_____

_____

_____

_____

Annual or Sessional Professional Growth Plans

"Let bygones be bygones" describes some people's philosophy for life, but in our opinion these words should not guide teachers within their professions. On New Year's Eve, many of us reflect back on the passing year, re-evaluate, and make New Year's resolutions. Similarly, at the beginning of a new school year or session, it is valuable for us to reassess our teaching and set goals for professional growth.

Task 1

1. At the beginning of your next teaching year or session, review program areas in the following chart. At the end of the year or session, revisit the chart and fill in column 3. Focus on three areas and formulate your growth objectives.

Program area	Your objective	Results
Course outline		
Daily plans		
Handouts		
Field trips		
Guest speakers		
Classroom organization and arrangement		
Communication skills		
Class events		
Conferences, workshops		
New units or topics		
New resources		
Teaching skills to monitor		

Program area	Your objective	Results
Knowledge of the subject matter		
Other:		

2. How did the results match your objectives? What actions do you plan to take in your next teaching session?

_____

_____

_____

_____

Task 2

Portfolio assessment has secured its place in student evaluation but to date it has not been used systematically in teacher evaluation. Only occasionally does one come across an article describing how the process is conducted in some programs, where attempts are made to broaden options for teacher self-evaluation by adding a portfolio component. This technique can also be used as part of peer-monitoring projects or supervisory evaluation.

A portfolio represents an assortment of items that illustrate work accomplished during a school year or course. Teachers are encouraged to include material that represents both successful and unsuccessful teaching, so that ideas for improvement will be revealed along with creativity and strengths. The artifacts may be categorized according to the factors considered relevant for program evaluation as conducted by a particular school board, program administration, or school. They can be reviewed by the teacher alone or by a supervisor as part of an evaluation or less formal constructive dialogue, or teachers may opt to share their collections with colleagues so that the process will benefit everyone. Supervisory or peer evaluation of portfolios, if conducted sensitively, provides the opportunity for teachers to share their rationale for particular actions or activities and to exchange advice and suggestions.

Like other techniques, portfolios are most effective for evaluative purposes if they are used in conjunction with other approaches. Completing a checklist related to long-range plans or watching a video of yourself in action in the classroom in order to analyze particular teaching skills could be done alongside the gathering and reviewing of artifacts. The main underlying principle, as with any other self-evaluation technique, is awareness raising.

This task will help you create and monitor a portfolio. At the beginning of the year, designate a file box for your portfolio collection. Label it clearly so it will not be accidentally discarded, and put it somewhere easily accessible. Throughout the year or session, gather artifacts related to your class or program and store them in the box. To make the whole process more systematic, prepare a portfolio review chart such as the one shown below. Keep the chart in the box, and make a note each time you add an artifact.

Topic	Artifacts	Reflections
Course outline		
Daily plans		
Handouts		
Student work		
"Souvenirs" from field trips		
Materials depicting class events		
Visual aids		
Materials collected at conferences or workshops		
Handouts from guest speakers		
New units, topics developed		
New resources tried out		
Knowledge of the subject matter		
Other: _____		
_____		
_____		
_____		
_____		

1. Toward the end of the year, set up a session for reflection with a colleague or a supervisor. Ask him or her to look through your portfolio while you discuss what you have accomplished, share any concerns, and seek advice. What is the result? What have you learned about the process? What insights have you gained that you can apply in your next teaching session?

_____

_____

_____

_____

2. Compare your objectives set at the beginning of the session or year and the results revealed by your portfolio contents. How do the two compare? What conclusions can you draw?

_____

_____

3. Use your reflections from this task and the preceding one to set up professional development objectives for next year or session.

_____

_____

_____

_____

Developing Knowledge of the Subject Matter: Focus on Language Teaching

> _Knowledge is of two kinds. We know a subject ourselves,_
> _or we know where we can find information upon it._
> SAMUEL JOHNSON, IN BOSWELL'S
> _THE LIFE OF SAMUEL JOHNSON_

Part of professional development is ensuring that we remain current with developments within our own disciplines. Our expertise is in language teaching, and we offer the following tasks for our colleagues in this area.

Finding a good balance between time allotted to working on methodology and to developing discipline-related knowledge is difficult. Consider the following account:

A teacher recently arrived in Canada from Europe was called to supply teach in a grade 3/4 class. As usual, she found a little note from the regular teacher on the desk. Among other instructions, there was a sentence that read, "If the weather is nice, take the kids outside for their phys. ed. time. They can play soccer baseball." Soccer baseball? Having taught ESL/EFL throughout her career, she had never heard of soccer baseball and certainly didn't know how to play it. In a panic, she ran to the teacher next door, explained the problem, and cried for help. The teacher reassured her by saying, "No reason to worry. The kids know how to play it."

The class went outside and the kids showed her the way to the field. Judging by their actions, she realized that two teams had to be created. This was accomplished, and the teams started to play. The teacher could not make head or tail of what the students were doing. She had absolutely no idea why they were running, who was playing against whom, or what they were supposed to do to score. The game went surprisingly well for several minutes, but then an argument erupted about whether one team had scored. Obviously, the teacher could not provide the answers to the students' questions, so she pointed at random to one team. That created a bout of rage among members of the other team, and she gathered that her decision had not been just. The scenario was repeated several times. Furious and frustrated, the kids started yelling, and some refused to play. At that moment the teacher realized that the principal was looking out the window. "Well, that's good-bye to my career as a supply teacher," she thought to herself.

We should always analyze our actions in terms of the consequences for our students. In the preceding scenario, playing soccer baseball was supposed to have been a pleasant, relaxed time for physical activity, after which the students would return to class energized to tackle the "intellectual stuff." Instead, they came back frustrated, annoyed, and feeling hostile toward their teacher. The lesson to be learned is that honesty about mastery (or lack of it) of the subject matter is the best policy. It is not unusual, however, for inexperienced teachers or those suffering from a lack of self-confidence to feel that they will lose face if they admit to a "deficiency."

No one can know everything, but teachers do need to have adequate knowledge of what they teach. "Adequate" could be defined as the amount of knowledge needed to deal effectively with the demands of the current teaching situation. In language teaching, being a native speaker does not guarantee adequate knowledge. Indeed, some native speakers may be poor writers, lack an understanding of grammar, or be slow, inefficient readers or speakers with limited vocabulary and poor command of register. On the other hand, non-native speakers may have difficulty with local idioms and expressions.

Task 1

1. How would you rate your own proficiency in the following areas?

Area	Very solid	Solid	Fair	Weak
Speaking/listening skills				
Grammar				
Pronunciation				
Vocabulary				
Idioms				
Spelling				
Reading skills				
Writing skills				

2. What can you do to improve your skills in any areas you rated fair or weak?

_____

_____

_____

_____

Task 2

If you are not a native speaker of the language you teach but live and work in a country where that language is spoken, you probably consider yourself lucky because of the many opportunities you have to develop your proficiency. If, however, you live in a country where the language you teach is not spoken, your deficiencies in that language may trouble you because you do not have adequate opportunity to work on them.

1. How do you feel about your language proficiency? Are you merely maintaining it, or are you improving it?

_____

_____

2. How much chance do you have to interact with native speakers of the language you teach?

_____

_____

3. If you are a non-native speaker of the language you teach, do you teach in a setting where the students and staff speak primarily your own first language? If so, how do you feel this may be affecting your proficiency in the target language?

_____

_____

4. Do you take time to study and develop knowledge of the language you teach?

_____

_____

5. If you are a non-native speaker, do you feel you spend more time on preparation compared to native speakers? If so, how do you feel about it?

_____

_____

6. Do this task if you are not completely content with your level of proficiency in the language you teach. Which of the following things are you now doing or planning to do to improve your proficiency?

	Now doing	Planning to do
I take courses in the language.		
I attend workshops or presentations.		

246

	Now doing	Planning to do
I consciously work on building vocabulary.		
I continually seek interaction with native speakers.		
I have a native-speaking "monitor" who gives me feedback and correction.		
I invite native-speaking volunteers into my program to facilitate my own and my students' language development.		
I systematically read and write in the target language.		
I systematically listen to the radio, watch television, or read newspapers in the target language.		
I consciously analyze the language of newspapers and magazines.		
I tape radio/TV broadcasts and analyze the language used.		

7. How do you plan to undertake the activities you indicated you were not already doing?

_____

_____

_____

_____

Appendix: Using Video- or Audiotaping Seeing Yourself as Others See You

If you want to reflect on how you feel about your teaching, write reflective notes after each lesson; if you are ready to hear objective comments about your teaching, invite an observer to your classroom. But if you want to gain the most realistic image of your teaching practice, record yourself, play the tape back, and self-evaluate.

Audio- or videorecording of lessons is invaluable for all teachers—novice and experienced alike—who are interested in improving their skills. Indeed, videorecording followed by individual or group viewing and analysis is used in pre- and inservice teacher training programs around the world. It allows us to explore both our effective and our ineffective classroom behaviors, to congratulate ourselves on our strengths, and to determine what needs to be done to make our teaching even better.

I [Vesna] am currently involved in directing a video self-evaluation project with my colleagues Lisa Morgan and Michael Galli. In the spring of 1998 we invited adult ESL instructors in the Toronto Catholic District School Board to participate in piloting the project, designed to help them reflect on their teaching practice and results. Hanna and I developed procedures to be used with the participants, and these were reviewed by Lisa and Michael before we began our experiment. Even though the project is still under way and data are not yet available, the majority of participating teachers have indicated that they find the stuctured technique useful and effective. They report having received insights into their classroom management and interaction, body language, use of teaching aids, and so on. In most cases, analysis of their tapes assisted them in discovering classroom behaviors they were not aware of. Participants have also described the videotaping technique as intrinsically motivating and have said that it boosted their confidence in their teaching. They have also suggested that it could be combined with peer evaluation or become part of department- or school-wide evaluation projects.

In this chapter, we provide an overview of the value of taping in self-evaluation. (Note that although we generally refer to videotaping, we realize that video equipment is not available in all programs, schools, or districts. In these cases, audiorecording can be used to almost equal effect.) We also describe the procedures for taping, viewing, and analysis that have been adopted in our pilot project and provide a photocopiable master of our "Video/Audio Self-Evaluation Package for Teachers," which readers are welcome to reproduce.

An Effective Technique

The experts agree that recording of our work in the classroom yields numerous benefits:
- It facilitates self-evaluation.
- It raises our awareness of the strengths and weaknesses of our teaching practices.
- It provides the opportunity to observe students and student-teacher interaction.
- It allows us to re-examine decisions we made when planning and preparing the lesson we taped.
- It gives us the chance to challenge and re-examine our assumptions and expectations about teaching.
- It enhances professional development.

To be effective, however, recording and evaluation of lessons must be done systematically. Consider the following scenario:

A language teacher videotaped herself during a three-hour lesson. Her impression upon playing back the tape for the first time was that the lesson had flowed smoothly. She felt that her listening skills during teacher-student interaction were strong, and she noticed that she was allowing a longer wait time between her questions and the students' responses than she had thought. In addition, she picked up some details she had not been conscious of during the lesson—students' facial expressions as they worked in groups, their and her own body language, and so on.

A week later, she played the tape again. This time, she focused on her interaction with students and conducted a detailed analysis of what the tape revealed about that aspect of her teaching practice. When she wrote up a transcript of a ten-minute segment of class discussion, she discovered that the interaction was not really as smooth as she had originally thought. She realized that she had cut off students or interrupted them unnecessarily on several occasions. The result was that student responses were shorter than they could have been, and that some students had not been given a chance to express themselves at all. Also, she found that most of her questions were of the type to generate only a yes or no answer, and they did not give students the opportunity to elaborate on their ideas.

This episode reveals a cautionary note about this approach to self-evaluation: taping does not yield beneficial results in terms of insight into practice if teachers simply play back the tape without focus or critical thought. A systematic and objective exploration of the information in the recording is required, followed by a detailed analysis of both the tape's content and its implications for future practice.

As you play back a tape several times, you assume the role of both assessor and "assessee," and you are put in the position of being able to draw conclusions from both perspectives. Adopting a supervisory point of view, you might ask how effective your actions were. How beneficial was your lesson for the students? How much knowledge did they gain? How appropriate were your interchanges with them? At the same time, because you are the teacher, you can provide a rationale for your actions. What were your intentions in a certain segment of the lesson? Are the reasons behind your actions strong enough to support them? This dual perspective allows you truly to identify the actions that most benefit your students.

Hypothesis Development Technique

We created the Hypothesis Development Technique (HDP) for gathering and analyzing video data for the Toronto Catholic District School Board self-evaluation project. With HDP, the teacher is guided through several viewings or listenings of a tape, and focuses on a different, more challenging task during each one. The objective is to help the teacher identify a specific aspect of his or her practice for analysis, determine the effective and ineffective behaviors associated with it, draw conclusions, and develop an action plan for improvement. By narrowing the focus to one teaching area only, teachers are able to see more clearly what needs to be adapted, changed, or corrected.

The Hypothesis Development Technique assumes that the ability to evaluate the implication of an action depends on the ability to foresee the implication of a different action. For example, if a teacher has asked an open-ended question instead of one that requires only a yes or no response, what would be the impact on classroom communication? If an activity were shorter, would students' interest level be higher and more sustained?

Despite the fact that HDP analyzes one aspect of teaching, it remains a holistic approach: it leads teachers first through a global assessment of a lesson and then to identification of particulars, thereby keeping track of the overall value of the lesson and the role of the segment within it.

The procedure itself is outlined in detail in the Video/Audio Self-Evaluation Package for Teachers that concludes this chapter. In brief, HDP follows these steps:

1. *First viewing.* How does the segment captured on tape differ from the perception you had about it in class?

2. *Second viewing.* Different parts of the lesson—and therefore different segments of the tape—highlight different aspects of teaching and classroom interaction. Does any area of teaching leap out for analysis? If so, transcribe the segment that highlights it.

3. *Third viewing.* Assess the effectiveness of your actions. What would have been the impact of a different action? What would you like to change? What role does the segment play in the overall effectiveness of your lesson?

4. *Follow-up.* After a week or two, make a new recording. Compare your actions in the new recording with those in the old.

The steps and techniques described in what follows can be carried out in individual or group settings. Options for implementing self-evaluation by mixing and matching different techniques are endless: all you need is the determination to start!

Video/Audio Self-Evaluation Package for Teachers

Recording your teaching practice offers by far the most objective illustration of your skills. Supervisors, colleagues, or students can provide feedback or comments related to your teaching, but nothing is more beneficial than making a tape so that your supervisory self can watch or listen to your teaching self. The following material has been developed to guide you as you undertake this form of self-evaluation.

Technical Aspects

1. Explain to your students the purpose of the taping exercise. Obtain their permission to be taped the day before, and ask them to sign a consent form if this is required in your program.

2. In the event you are *audiotaping* yourself, use a miniature tape-recorder (preferably one with a pop-up microphone) you can carry around. This will provide the best results, but if such a machine is not available, use an ordinary tape-recorder with a built-in microphone, and experiment first to find the best spot in the classroom to position it. Make sure you use high-quality cassette tapes.

3. If you are *videotaping*

- Position the camera to the side of the class rather than at the back, to allow a view of both learners and teacher.
- Do not point the camera at windows or place it directly in front of them.
- Experiment to find the position that yields the best picture, sound, and view of most of the class.
- For stability and safety, use a tripod.
- A stationary camera will in most cases show only part of the classroom, and most teachers find that they need a student to act as a camera operator to obtain a tape that will provide a view of the whole class—introduce the camera first and teach a lesson on how to use it, providing students with some time to practice.

4. To ensure a smooth start, press the record button several minutes prior to the beginning of your lesson.

5. Remember that it will take you and your students several minutes to forget about the camera or tape-recorder and act naturally. Do not use the start-up segment of your lesson for later analysis.

6. Record longer segments of your lessons.

Playback Procedures

There are many possible procedures that could be followed when undertaking self-evaluation with video- or audiorecording. The method suggested here is based on analyzing, in detail, one teaching area only, and could be compared to conducting a cumulative activity in the classroom, during which students are given a series of tasks that gradually increase in complexity.

First Playback

In your first viewing of or listening to the tape you recorded in your classroom, your focus should be on determining how different the lesson was from the perceptions you had of it while you were teaching.

1. Play back the tape with a single objective in mind: getting a general idea of what has been taped. It may shed light on elements of your teaching you were not really aware of—students' and your own body language, reactions, etc.

2. Ask yourself, "How does my perception of what happened in the classroom differ from what I can see or hear on the tape?" Take notes if you wish. At this stage in the process, teachers in our program have jotted down comments such as "The language that I use when I teach seems to be a bit too informal," "I shouldn't drink coffee while I teach—it looks so unprofessional," and "I watched my tape till two o'clock one night—it was so interesting I simply could not stop watching it. Among other things, I noticed that I was interacting much more with students on one side of the classroom (I had not realized that before), so I decided that needed to be corrected."

Second Playback

At this point it is time to make a decision about the aspect of teaching you want to focus on. Different parts of the lesson—and therefore different segments of the tape—highlight different aspects of teaching and classroom interaction. Each recorded segment of a lesson usually lends itself to the analysis of at least one particular aspect.

1. Place a checkmark next to the area that you would like to work on.

— classroom set up
— voice projection and control
— body language
— my position and movement in class
— awareness of learners
— use and distribution of materials and aids
— lesson transitions
— pacing and timing
— student participation
— student-teacher rapport
— classroom interaction:
    — teacher talk
    — student talk
    — teacher-student interaction
    — student-student interaction
    — students' individual work
    — pair work

— group work
    — teacher questions and student responses
    — giving instructions
— procedures
— feedback and correction

2. Determine whether you need to analyze an entire tape or long segment or if you can focus on a shorter subsegment.

3. Transcribe at least one short segment for analysis. Transcripts of classroom interaction seem to reveal considerably more than mere viewing or listening, especially if you are analyzing any interaction-related aspect of teaching.

4. Analyze the transcript in terms of the appropriateness of your actions and behaviors pertaining to the particular aspect of teaching you are working on, keeping in mind your learners and their needs.

5. Finally, determine your overall impression of your skills. If you were an observer or a supervisor, how would you rate your level of skill?

    5   4   3   2   1
Very effective   Not effective

If you were a student in the class, how meaningful would you have found the lesson?

    5   4   3   2   1
Very meaningful   Not meaningful

Third Playback

Conduct a systematic analysis of your actions by filling in the two self-evaluation forms at the end of this section. The objective is to identify particular teacher behaviors that trigger positive or negative learner behaviors. Base your analysis on these key questions:

- What is done effectively?
- What could have been done differently?
- What impact would a different decision or action have had on your lesson or on class communication?
- What conclusions can you draw?
- What is your action plan?

In addition, think in terms of the appropriateness of your actions, the impact they had on classroom work or learners, and the possible implications of different actions.

Video/Audio Self-Evaluation Form 1 is designed to help you analyze an effective teacher behavior captured on your tape. If, for example, a teacher hoped to analyze her skills in giving instructions, she might play back the tape and note in the "Action" column that her instructions for a particular task were clear and concise. The result was that students were on task quickly without feeling the need to ask for clarification. Her conclusion might be that effective delivery of instructions in that particular case depended on waiting for students' attention, using visual clues and providing examples, and checking that students had understood.

Video/Audio Self-Evaluation Form 2 is intended to help teachers identify a behavior from the recording that needs to be changed and to develop an action plan for improvement. If the focus area were classroom interaction, for example, the teacher might note from the tape that he interrupted his students while they were speaking on two occasions. In the "Rationale" column he might indicate that his interruptions were intended to offer clarification and to help students express themselves, but the tape actually revealed something different for the "Result" column: students were frustrated at not being given the chance to formulate their own thoughts and expressions. The teacher's hypothesis would then detail what would have happened had he not interrupted—perhaps students' responses would have been more detailed, and they would have felt that he was genuinely interested in what they had to say. The action plan might be to make a conscious effort not to interrupt, and to tape another lesson to see if improvement has been realized.

Follow-Up

Tape yourself again after one or two weeks and evaluate the same aspect of your teaching. Compare the two tapes and determine how and to what extent you have improved the behavior you identified as problematic or ineffective. If you were an observer or supervisor, how would you rate your level of skill this time?

    5   4   3   2   1
Very effective   Not effective

If you feel it might be beneficial, tape yourself a third (or even a fourth) time and reassess your behavior.

Checklist for Video- or Audiorecording

1. Obtain student permission (and, if required, signed consent forms).

2. Work out technical considerations.

3. Play the tape back to determine how what was recorded differs from perceptions.

4. Play the tape back again and decide on an area for detailed analysis.

5. Transcribe a short segment.

6. Analyze the transcript in terms of appropriateness of actions depicted on the tape.

7. Determine how effective that teaching aspect is, adopting the point of view of both a supervisor and learners.

255

8. Play the tape back again. Identify effective behaviors and fill out Video/Audio Self-Evaluation Form 1.

9. Identify behaviors that require improvement and complete Video/Audio Self-Evaluation Form 2.

10. Establish an action plan.

11. Make a second recording one to two weeks after the first.

12. Evaluate the same aspect of teaching on both tapes and compare the first and second recordings.

Video/Audio Self-Evaluation Form 1:
Effective Teacher Behaviors

Length of segment analyzed: _____ minutes
Teaching aspect analyzed: _____

Action/behavior	How many times?	Result	Conclusions

Video/Audio Self-Evaluation Form 2:
Teacher Behaviors That Require Improvement

Length of segment analyzed: _____ minutes
Teaching aspect analyzed: _____

Action/behavior	How many times?	Rationale	Result: What was the impact?	Hypothesis: What would be the impact of a different action?	Action plan

Bibliography

Ashton-Warner, S. *Teacher*. New York: Simon & Schuster, 1965.

Barer-Stein, T. & J.A. Draper. *The Craft of Teaching Adults*. Toronto: Culture Concepts, 1988.

Bell, J. *Teaching Multilevel Classes in ESL*. San Diego, CA: Dominie Press, 1988.

Brown, H.D. *Teaching by Principles*. Englewood Cliffs, NJ: Prentice Hall, 1994.

Brown, J.D. *The Elements of Language Curriculum. A Systematic Approach to Program Development*. Rowley, MA: Newbury House, 1995.

Budd Rowe, M. "Wait Time: Slowing down May Be a Way of Speeding Up!" In *Journal of Teacher Education*. January-February 1986.

Cabaj, H. & V. Nikolic. "Questions Teachers Ask Themselves: From Reflective to Effective Teacher." In *TESL Contact*. Vol. 24, no. 2 (1998).

Celce-Murcia, M. "Grammar Pedagogy in Second and Foreign Language Learning." In *TESOL Quarterly*. Vol. 25, no. 3 (1991).

Chemali, J. "Personal Skills of an ESL Teacher." In *TESL Contact*. Vol. 23, no. 2 (1997).

Engkent, L.P. "Real People Don't Talk Like Books: Teaching Colloquial English." In *TESL Canada Journal*. Vol. 4, special issue (1986).

Eyring, J.L. "What's an Objective Anyway?" In *TESL Canada Journal*. Vol. 15, no. 2 (1998).

Freeman, D. "Observing Teachers: Three Approaches to In-Service Training and Development." In *TESOL Quarterly*. Vol. 16, no. 1 (1982).

Freeman, D. "Teacher Training, Development and Decision Making: A Model of Teaching and Related Strategies for Language Teacher Education." In *TESOL Quarterly*. Vol. 23, no. 1 (1989).

Freeman, D. *Doing Teacher Research*. Toronto: Heinle & Heinle, 1998.

Golebiowska, A. *Getting Students to Talk* (International English Language Teaching series). Englewood Cliffs, NJ: Prentice Hall, 1990.

Gurdek, J. *Materials Evaluation Survey*. Toronto: Metropolitan Separate School Board, 1996.

Harmer, J. "Taming the Big 'I': Teacher Performance and Student Satisfaction." In *ELT Journal*. Vol. 49, no. 4 (1995).

Hart, F.R. "Teachers Observing Teachers. Evaluation." In H.J. Broderick (Ed.), *Teaching at an Urban University*. Boston, MA: Center for the Improvement of Teaching, University of Massachusetts, 1987.

Ho, B. "Using Lesson Plans as a Means of Reflection." In *ELT Journal*. Vol. 49, no. 1 (1995).

Johnson, K. "Mistake Correction." In *ELT Journal*. Vol. 42, no. 2 (1988).

Katchen, J. "Using Star T.V. in the Classroom: A Potpourri of Ideas." Paper presented at the Annual International Meeting of the Institute of Language in Education, Hong Kong (15–19 Dec. 1993). ERIC. Document Reproduction Service No. ED 366 221.

Katchen, J. "Learning to Listen to Authentic English from Satellite TV." Paper presented at the Annual Meeting of the Thai Teachers of English to Speakers of Other Languages, Bangkok, Thailand (13–15 Jan. 1994). ERIC Document Reproduction Service No. ED 366 222.

Long, M.H. & J.C. Richards (Eds.). *Methodology in TESOL.* Boston, MA: Heinle & Heinle, 1987.

Long, M.H. & C.J. Sato. "Classroom Foreigner Talk Discourse: Forms and Functions of Teachers' Questions." In H.W. Seliger & M.H. Long (Eds.), *Classroom Oriented Research in Secondary Language Acquisition.* Rowley, MA: Newbury House, 1983.

Lowe, T. "An Experiment in Role Reversal: Teachers as Language Learners." In *ELT Journal.* Vol. 41, no. 2 (1987).

Lund, R. "A Taxonomy for Teaching Second Language Listening." In *Foreign Language Annals.* Vol. 23, no. 2 (1990).

Mendelsohn, David J. "There ARE Strategies for Listening." In *TEAL Occasional Papers*, no. 8 (1984).

Mendelsohn, David J. "Making the Speaking Class a Real Learning Experience: The Keys to Teaching Spoken English." In *TESL Canada Journal.* Vol. 10, no. 1 (1992).

Morgan, J. & M. Rinvolucri. *Vocabulary.* Oxford, UK: Oxford University Press, 1986.

Nunan, D. "Communicative Language Teaching—Making It Work." In *ELT Journal.* Vol. 41, no. 2 (1987).

Nunan, D. *Designing Tasks for the Communicative Classroom.* Cambridge, UK: Cambridge University Press, 1989.

Nunan, D. & C. Lamb. *The Self-Directed Teacher.* Cambridge, UK: Cambridge University Press, 1996.

Nunan, D. & R. Oxford. "Understanding and Implementing a Task-Based Approach to Language Teaching." Paper presented at the annual meeting of the Teachers of English to Speakers of Other Languages (TESOL), Chicago, IL (March 1996).

O'Neill, R. "The Myth of Learner-Centredness: Or the Importance of Doing Ordinary Things Well." In *ELT Journal.* Vol. 45, no. 4 (1991).

Oxford, R. *Language Learning Strategies: What Every Teacher Should Know.* Rowley, MA: Newbury House, 1990.

Pennington, M.C. & V. Stevens. *Computers in Applied Linguistics: An International Perspective.* Clevedon, UK: Multilingual Matters, 1992.

Prabhu, N.S. "The Dynamics of the Language Lesson." In *TESOL Quarterly.* Vol. 26, no. 2 (1992).

Prodromou, L. "The Good Language Teacher." In *English Teaching Forum.* Vol. 29, no. 4 (April 1991).

Richards, J.C. "The Dilemma of Teacher Education in TESOL." In *TESOL Quarterly.* Vol. 21, no. 2 (1987).

Richards, J.C. *The Language Teaching Matrix.* Cambridge, UK: Cambridge University Press, 1990.

Richards, J.C. *The Context of Language Teaching.* Cambridge, UK: Cambridge University Press, 1991.

Richards, J.C. & D. Nunan (Eds.). *Second Language Teacher Education.* Cambridge, UK: Cambridge University Press, 1990.

Underhill, A. "The Psychological Atmosphere We Create in Our Classrooms." In *The Language Teacher Online*. September 1997.

Ur, P. *A Course in Language Teaching: Practice and Theory*. Cambridge, UK: Cambridge University Press, 1996.

Wajnryb, R. *Classroom Observation Tasks*. Cambridge, UK: Cambridge University Press, 1993.

Wells, G. et al. *Changing Schools from Within*. Portsmouth, NH: Heinemann, 1994.

Bibliography

Additional Resources

Airasian, P.W. & Gullickson, A.R. *Teacher Self-Evaluation Tool Kit.* Thousand Oaks, CA: Corwin Press, 1997.

Allwright, D. "What Do We Want Teaching Materials For?" In *ELT Journal.* Vol. 36, no. 1 (1981).

Allwright, D. "Quality and Sustainability in Teacher Research." In *TESOL Quarterly.* Vol. 31, no. 2 (1997).

Allwright, D. & K.M. Bailey. *Focus on the Language Classroom.* Cambridge, UK: Cambridge University Press, 1991.

Assinder, W. "Peer Teaching—Peer Learning: One Model." In *ELT Journal.* Vol. 45, no. 3 (1991).

Bluestein, J.E. *Being a Successful Teacher. A Practical Guide to Instruction and Management.* Carthage, IL: Fearon Teacher Aids, 1989.

Cabaj, H. "Models of Use of Computers in Language Teaching and Learning." In *TESL Contact.* Vol. 24, no. 2 (1998).

Cabaj, H. & V. Nikolic. *Self-Evaluation Tasks.* Toronto: Metropolitan Separate School Board, 1998.

Cohen, H. "Teaching Improvement and Teacher Evaluation." In H.J. Broderick (Ed.), *Teaching at an Urban University.* Boston, MA: Center for the Improvement of Teaching, University of Massachusetts, 1987.

Gebhard, J.G. "Models of Supervision: Choices." In *TESOL Quarterly.* Vol. 18, no. 3 (1984).

Gitlin, A. & J. Smith. "Toward Educative Forms of Teacher Education." In *Educational Theory.* Vol. 40, no. 1 (1990).

Golombek, P.R. "A Study of Language Teachers' Personal Practical Knowledge." In *TESOL Quarterly.* Vol. 32, no. 3 (1998).

Gunter, P.L. & T.M. Reed. "Self-Evaluation of Instruction: A Protocol for Functional Assessment of Teacher Behaviour." In *Intervention in School and Clinic.* Vol. 31, no. 4 (1996).

Haertel, G.D. *A Primer on Teacher Self-Evaluation* (Publication series No. 93-3). Washington, DC: Office of Educational Research and Improvement, U.S. Department of Education, 1993.

Hawkey, K. "Learning from Peers: The Experience of Student Teachers in School-Based Teacher Education." In *Journal of Teacher Education.* Vol. 46, no. 1 (1995).

Hayes, D. "In-Service Teacher Development: Some Basic Principles." In *ELT Journal.* Vol. 49, no. 3 (1995).

Johnston, B. "Do EFL Teachers Have Careers?" In *TESOL Quarterly*. Vol. 31, no. 4 (1997).

Kilbourn, B. "Self-Monitoring in Teaching." In *American Educational Research Journal*. Vol. 28, no. 4 (1991).

Koehler, M. "Self-Assessment in the Evaluation Process." In *NASSP Bulletin* September 1990.

Kurtz, K. "It's in the Box: Portfolio Power for Teacher Evaluation." In *The Executive Educator*. February 1996.

Laycock, J. & P. Bunnag. "Developing Teacher Self-Awareness: Feedback and the Use of Video." In *ELT Journal*. Vol. 45, no. 1 (1991).

Mackay, R., S. Wellesley, & E. Bazergan. "Participatory Evaluation." In *ELT Journal*. Vol. 49, no. 4 (1995).

Metropolitan Separate School Board. *MSSB Model for Appraisal, Growth and Improvement in Teaching Practices*. Toronto: 1992.

Rolheiser, C. (Ed.). *Self-Evaluation and Helping Students Get Better at It!* Toronto: Clear Group (Durham Board of Education and the Ontario Institute for Studies in Education), 1996.

Schwartz, J.E. "How Can We Evaluate Ourselves?" In *Arithmetic Teacher*. February 1992.

Setteducatti, D. "Portfolio Assessment for Teachers: A Reflection on the Farmingdale [Model]." In *Journal of Staff Development*. Vol. 16, no. 3 (1995).

Tirri, K. "Evaluating Teacher Effectiveness by Self-Assessment: A Cross-Cultural Study" (Research Rep. No. 122). Helsinki, Finland: Helsinki University, Department of Teacher Education, 1993.

Widdowson, H.G. "The Roles of Teacher and Learner." In *ELT Journal*. Vol. 41, no. 2 (1987).

Zeichner, K.M. "Preparing Reflective Teachers: An Overview of Instructional Strategies Which Have Been Employed in Pre-Service Teacher Education." In *International Journal of Educational Research*. Vol. 11, no. 5 (1987).